Discussions of Alexander Pope

DISCUSSIONS OF LITERATURE

General Editor JOSEPH H. SUMMERS, Washington University

Edited by

Hamlet	J. C. LEVENSON, University of Minnesota
Alexander Pope	RUFUS A. BLANSHARD, University of Connecticut
The Novel	ROGER SALE, Amherst College
George Eliot	RICHARD STANG, Carleton College
Moby-Dick	MILTON R. STERN, University of Connecticut

DISCUSSIONS

OF

ALEXANDER POPE

Edited with an Introduction by

Rufus A. Blanshard

THE UNIVERSITY OF CONNECTICUT

D. C. Heath and Company

BOSTON

CONTENTS

INTRODUCTION

"CRITICISM on the poet's works has been exhausted: his position as an English classic has long been fixed." If so, much of this book represents a remarkable second wind. Robert Carruthers, Pope's biographer of a century ago, may be excused for not having predicted modern literary criticism, but he was hardly right even about his own age. What *was* Pope's fixed position as an English classic? Warton (his ostensible detractor) had put him "*next* to Milton, and *just* above Dryden." Johnson (his staunch defender) had put him just *below* Dryden. Wordsworth, who was suspiciously intimate with the works of Dryden and Pope, cried a plague on both: "their way," he said, "lies almost at the foot of Parnassus." Hazlitt and De Quincey even found Pope *incorrect*. It was not a long fall from there: "Dryden and Pope," wrote Arnold, the "Atticus" of his day, "are not classics of our poetry, they are classics of our prose." Was Carruthers perhaps begging the question about his "English classic"— was Pope Great but No Poet? Warton had implied this, Johnson had denied it, and the two schools of nineteenth-century Pope criticism were founded. The second was more of a cell than a school, but it had a zealous leader in Byron: "Taking passage for passage, I will undertake to cite more lines teeming with *imagination* from Pope than from any *two* living poets, be they who they may." Here is Arnold's touchstone method long before Arnold, to prove an opposite point. Byron, looking backward, anticipated modern taste: T. S. Eliot, the Arnold of his day, has summed it up in three words, "Pope is poetry." Even so, can it be said that Pope's position—or Mr.

Eliot's, for that matter—is now "fixed"? Not long ago F. W. Bateson, himself one of the editors of the great Twickenham Edition of Pope's poems, mentioned Mr. Eliot somewhat unflatteringly, and went on to call Pope "another minor poet with occasional brilliances." This is the same Mr. Bateson who, as editor, had written feelingly, "How his editors and biographers have hated Pope." Criticism, apparently, has not been exhausted.

Nor was Carruthers lucky as a biographer, though he was a good one and did not hate Pope. New light on Pope's life was just then being shed by C. W. Dilke, and even a revised edition of his book could not make the adjustment. Then came the monumental Elwin-Courthope edition of Pope's works, and it too, almost immediately, was found wanting. It was as though Pope himself, refusing to stay put, had popped up to score a few more Dunces. Our own age, partly to avoid that fate, has been cautious about the "facts." The best biography to date, George Sherburn's, stopped at 1727 because one of the crucial sources for the later years, the correspondence, had yet to be satisfactorily edited—a prodigious task which only Professor Sherburn could (and recently did) complete. At the moment there doesn't *seem* to be much left to discover, but a "definitive" biography does not exist, and it would be rash to suppose it ever will. Pope the man, like his poetry, eludes final definition.

Short of that, however, there have been many notable estimates and descriptions of his poetry, and this book is a selection of them. So much had to be omitted, for lack of space, that it was easy to make the first editorial decision: no biography. It was none the less a pity, for in Pope's case the life presents more fascinating *critical* problems than usual. Today especially, when the vogue for "classical" objectivity and rhetorical technique has infected criticism with academic anemia, it is salutary to remind ourselves that Pope lived, and that he wrote himself into his work. Furthermore, some of the things that have attracted the best biographical comment and speculation, from the earliest attacks on Pope to the latest defense of him, would tease the least curious mind. What *were* his relations with Dennis, with Addison, with Lady Mary and Lord Hervey? Why did he falsify his correspondence? How much French—and Greek—did he really know? The most austere critic would like, if he were asked privately, to listen in on one of those sessions with Bolingbroke that led (just how?) to the *Essay on Man*. The least prying amateur psychoanalyst notes, if he does not know quite how to *use*, Pope's size and sickliness, his attachment to his mother, his predilection for insect imagery. All of that (or most of it) has been sacrificed here.

A more difficult but related decision was to include nothing (with one exception, Warton's essay) from books on Pope. This decision was aided by their general availability (except for Warton's), as well as by the abundance of shorter and less accessible studies. The magnitude (the enormity!) of the omission may be indicated by a list of authors since Carruthers: Leslie Stephen, W. J. Courthope, William H. Mead, "George Paston," Lytton Strachey, Austin Warren, Edith Sitwell, Emile Audra, George Sherburn, Geoffrey Tillotson (two books), R. K. Root, Norman Ault, W. L. MacDonald, D. M. Knight, Bonamy Dobrée, Ian Jack, G. Wilson Knight, R. W. Rogers, Rebecca Price Parkin, Aubrey L. Williams, and Reuben Brower. (Unwittingly, Professors Sherburn and Tillotson have helped the editor adhere to this part of his scheme by writing just what he wanted from them outside of their books.) Two thirds of the books have been published since 1930, one third since 1950. Statistics can be used to still a compiler's conscience. Such is the present interest in Pope, he can say, that nobody will take this collection as more than a supplement to the books.

The reader will note other sacrifices, not of books only. The list would be longer and more dazzling of writers who have said important things on Pope in small compass and have nevertheless been left out: Addison, Dennis, Spence, Young, and Warburton from the eighteenth century; De Quincey, Macaulay, Sainte-Beuve, Ruskin, Tennyson, Pattison, Taine, Montégut, and Birrell from the nineteenth; more names than all of these from the twentieth. What anthologist has not been forced to groan, "Here is *not* God's plenty"? But apology is negative and must yield to principle.

The three aims of this book are to represent the historical curve of Pope criticism, to cover the main aspects of Pope's poetry, and to be interesting. None of the pieces is unrepresentative of its age, and taken as a whole they show what the different ages have thought. One thing the collection demonstrates is the diversity of opinion *within* the separate periods: Johnson and Warton, Byron and Hazlitt, Conington and Arnold, Tillotson and Leavis— a series of pairings that would give pause to the lover of labels. In one way or another, the book also covers the chief kinds of poetry that Pope wrote, and the characteristic effects. If there is an emphasis in the later essays on the mature works and the satiric modes, it is because modern criticism has leaned that way. Finally, in the narrowest and most subjective sense of the word, every piece has been "interesting" to the editor—that is, sufficiently lively and illuminating to hold his attention after he had read a lot of Pope criticism old and new.

The arrangement is chronological. All

of the longer pieces but the last three are abbreviations or extracts, but this is not so bad as it sounds. The amount of cutting has varied: Warton's two volumes, for example, have been reduced to a longish essay, while Professors Ker and Tillotson have been only slightly trimmed. The biggest splicing operation, as distinct from cutting, has been performed on *Seven Types of Ambiguity*, in which Pope figures attractively but intermittently. The shorter pieces require no special explanation. From William Wycherley to James Reston people have made casual and provocative remarks about Pope (as he made them about others), and the inclusion of a smattering of them is not a violation of the editor's principles.

RUFUS A. BLANSHARD

Discussions of Alexander Pope

Alexander Pope

Jonathan Swift

from Verses on the Death of Dr. Swift

> In Pope, I cannot read a Line,
> But with a Sigh, I wish it mine:
> When he can in one Couplet fix
> More sense than I can do in Six:
> It gives me such a jealous Fit,
> I cry, Pox take him, and his Wit.

(1731) ; reprinted from *Gulliver's Travels and Other Writings,* ed. Ricardo Quintana, New York, Modern Library, 1958, p. 526.

Voltaire

Letter XXII [1]

MR. POPE . . . is, I believe, the most elegant, the most correct, and, what is much more, the most harmonious poet that England has had. He has reduced the harsh blare of the English trumpet to the sweet sound of the flute; one can translate him, because he is extremely clear, and because his subjects are for the most part general and belong to all nations. [Voltaire here translates into couplets, "with my usual freedom," the passage on Spleen and her attendants, *Rape of the Lock*, IV, 17–38.] . . .

The *Essay on Man* . . . seems to me the most beautiful didactic poem, the most useful, the most sublime, that has ever been done in any language. . . .

Since everything in it belonging to metaphysics has been thought in all times and by all civilized peoples, this system is very closely akin to that of Leibnitz, which holds that, of all possible worlds, God must have chosen the best, and that in this best, the irregularities of our globe and the stupidities of its inhabitants must have their place. It further resembles Plato's idea that in the infinite chain of beings, our earth, our body, our soul are among the necessary links. But neither Leibnitz nor Pope admits the changes which Plato imagines these links, our souls and bodies, to have gone through. Plato spoke like a poet in his barely intelligible prose; and Pope speaks like a philosopher in his admirable verse. He says that all has been from the beginning as it had to be, and as it is.

I was flattered, I confess, to see that he agreed with me in one thing which I had said several years before: "You are amazed that God made man so limited, so ignorant, so unhappy. Why are you not amazed that he did not make him more limited, more ignorant and more unhappy?" When a Frenchman and an Englishman think alike, they must be right.

Poème sur la loi naturelle

L'EXORDE [2]

Mais Pope approfondit ce qu'ils [Horace and Boileau] ont effleuré;
D'un esprit plus hardi, d'un pas plus assuré,
Il porta le flambeau dans l'abîme de l'être;
Et l'homme avec lui seul apprit à se connaître.
L'art quelquefois frivole, et quelquefois divin,
L'art des vers est, dans Pope, utile au genre humain. [3]

[1] From *Lettres Philosophiques, ou Lettres Anglaises* (1734, 1756) ; ed. Raymond Naves, Paris, Editions Garnier Frères, 1951, pp. 126, 256–257. (Translation by the present editor.)

[2] (1752) ; ibid., p. 258.

[3]

Poem on Natural Law: Exordium

But Pope plumbed what they [Horace and Boileau] skimmed:
With a bolder mind, a surer step,
He carried the torch into the abyss of being;
And with him alone man learned to know himself.
Sometimes frivolous, and sometimes divine,
The art of verse is, in Pope, useful to humanity.

Joseph Warton

An Essay on the Genius and Writings of Pope

I REVERE the memory of Pope, I respect and honour his abilities; but I do not think him at the head of his profession. In other words, in that species of poetry wherein Pope excelled, he is superior to all mankind: and I only say, that this species of poetry is not the most excellent one of the art. . . .

Nothing can be more judicious than the method he [Horace] prescribes, of trying whether any composition be essentially poetical or not; which is, to drop entirely the measures and numbers, and transpose and invert the order of the words: and in this unadorned manner to peruse the passage. If there be really in it a true poetical spirit, all your inversions and transpositions will not disguise and extinguish it; but it will retain its lustre, like a diamond, unset, and thrown back into the rubbish of the mine. Let us make a little experiment on the following well-known lines; "Yes, you despise the man that is confined to books, who rails at human kind from his study; tho' what he learns, he speaks; and may perhaps advance some general maxims, or may be right by chance. The coxcomb bird, so grave and so talkative, that cries whore, knave, and cuckold, from his cage, tho' he rightly call many a passenger, you hold him no philosopher. And yet, such is the fate of all extremes, men may be read too much, as well as books. We grow more partial, for the sake of the observer, to observations which we ourselves make; less so to written wisdom, because another's. Maxims are drawn from notions, and those from guess." [Cf. *Moral Essays*,

I, 1–14.] What shall we say of this passage?—Why, that it is most excellent sense, but just as poetical as the "Qui fit Maecenas" of the author who recommends this method of trial. Take ten lines of the Iliad, Paradise Lost, or even of the Georgics of Virgil, and see whether by any process of critical chymistry, you can lower and reduce them to the tameness of prose. You will find that they will appear like Ulysses in his disguise of rags, still a hero, tho' lodged in the cottage of the herdsman Eumaeus. . . .

Descriptive poetry was by no means the shining talent of Pope. This assertion may be manifested by the few images introduced in . . . [*Windsor Forest*], which are not equally applicable to any place whatsoever. Rural beauty in general, and not the peculiar beauties of the forest of Windsor, are here described. Nor are the sports of setting, shooting, and fishing, included between the ninety-third and one hundred and forty-sixth verses, to which the reader is referred, at all more appropriated. The stag-chase, that immediately follows, although some of the lines are incomparably good, is not so full, so animated, and so circumstantiated, as that of Somerville.

The digression that describes the demolition of the thirty villages by William the Conqueror, is well imagined; particularly,

Round broken columns clasping ivy twin'd,
O'er heaps of ruin stalk'd the stately hind;
The fox obscene to gaping tombs retires,
And savage howlings fill the sacred quires. . . .

Two vols., London, 1756, 1782. (The excerpts from the first volume—i.e., those up to the end of page 7— are reprinted here from the second edition, 1762. Certain typographical features of the original are not retained.)

The story of Lodona is prettily Ovidian; but there is scarcely a single incident in it, but what is borrowed from some transformation of Ovid. . . .

He slides with dexterity and address from speaking of the miseries of the civil war to the blessings of peace. Old Father Thames is raised, and acts, and speaks, with becoming dignity. And though the trite and obvious insignia of a river god are attributed, yet there is one circumstance in his appearance highly picturesque,

His sea-green mantle waving with the wind. . . .

The influences and effects of peace, and its consequence, a diffusive commerce, are expressed by selecting such circumstances, as are best adapted to strike the imagination by lively pictures; the selection of which chiefly constitutes true poetry. An historian or prose-writer might say, "Then shall the most distant nations croud into my port": a poet sets before your eyes "the ships of uncouth form," that shall arrive in the Thames;

And *feather'd* people croud my wealthy side;
And *naked* youths, and *painted* chiefs admire
Our speech, our colour, and our strange *attire*. . . .

In describing the dreadful inhabitants of the portal of hell, . . . Virgil has exhibited no images so lively and distinct, as these living figures painted by Pope, each of them with their proper insignia and attributes.

———Envy her own snakes shall feel,
And Persecution mourn his broken wheel;
There Faction roar, Rebellion bite her chain,
And gasping Furies thirst for blood in vain. . . .

I am afraid our author in the following passage has fallen into a fault very uncommon in his writings, a reflection that is very far-fetched and forced;

Here waving groves a chequer'd scene display,
And part admit, and part exclude the day;
As some coy nymph her lover's warm address
Nor quite indulges, nor can quite repress.

. . . The fallacy consists in giving design and artifice to the wood, as well as to the coquette; and in putting the light of the sun and the warmth of a lover on a level.

A pathetic reflection, properly introduced into a descriptive poem, will have greater force and beauty, and more deeply interest a reader, than a moral one. When Pope therefore has described a pheasant shot, he breaks out into a very masterly exclamation;

Ah! what avail his glossy varying dyes,
His purple crest, and scarlet-circled eyes,
The vivid green his shining plumes unfold,
His painted wings, and breast that flames with gold.

This exquisite picture heightens the distress, and powerfully excites the commiseration of the reader. . . .

We are now arrived at a poem [*Essay on Criticism*] of that species, for which our author's genius was particularly turned, the *didactic* and the *moral*; it is therefore, as might be expected, a masterpiece in its kind. . . . We are indeed amazed to find such a knowledge of the world, such a maturity of judgment, and such a penetration into human nature, as are here displayed, in so very young a writer as was Pope, when he produced this Essay; for he was not twenty years old. Correctness and a just taste, are usually not attained but by long practice and experience in any art; but a clear head, and strong sense were the characteristical qualities of our author; and every man soonest displays his radical excellencies. If his predominant talent be warmth and vigor of imagination, it will break out in fanciful and luxuriant descriptions, the colouring of which will perhaps be too rich and glowing. If his chief force lies in the understanding rather than in the imagination, it will soon appear by solid and manly observations on life or learning, expressed in a more chast and subdued style. The former will frequently be hurried into obscurity or turgidity, and a false grandeur of diction; the latter will seldom hazard a figure, whose usage is not already established, or an image beyond common life; will always be perspicuous if not elevated; will never disgust, if not transport, his readers; will avoid the grosser faults, if not arrive at the greater beauties of composition. . . .

> Some neither can for wits nor critics pass,
> As heavy mules are neither horse nor ass;
> Those half-learn'd witlings, numerous in our isle,
> As half-form'd insects on the banks of Nile;
> Unfinish'd things, one knows not what to call,
> Their generation's so equivocal.

These lines and those preceding, and following them, are excellently satirical; and were, I think, the first we find in his works, that give an indication of that species of poetry to which his talent was most powerfully bent, and in which, tho' not, as we shall see, in others, he excelled all mankind. The simile of the mule heightens the satire, and is new; as is the application of the insects of the Nile. Pope never shines so brightly as when he is proscribing bad authors. . . .

> Thus Pegasus, a nearer way to take,
> May boldly deviate from the common track;
> From vulgar bounds with brave disorder part,
> And snatch a grace beyond the reach of art,
> Which, without passing thro' the judgment, gains
> The heart, and all it's ends at once obtains.

Here is evidently a blameable mixture of metaphors; where the attributes of the horse and the writer are confounded. The former may justly be said to "take a nearer way, and, to deviate from a track"; but how can a *horse* "snatch a grace," or "gain the heart"? . . .

[The simile of the Alps] is frequently mentioned, as an instance of the strength of fancy. The images however appear too general and indistinct, and the last line conveys no new idea to the mind. . . .

A needless Alexandrine ends the song.

Dryden was the first who introduced the frequent use of this measure into our English heroic, for we do not ever find it even in the longer works of Sandys, nor in Waller. Dryden has often used it very happily, and it gives a complete harmony to many of his triplets. By scrupulously avoiding it, Pope has fallen into an unpleasing and tiresome monotony in his Iliad. . . .

If the Moderns have excelled the Ancients in any species of writing, it seems to be in satire: and, particularly in that kind of satire, which is conveyed in the form of the epopee, a pleasing vehicle of satire, seldom, if ever, used by the ancients; for we know so little of the Margites of Homer, that it cannot be produced as an example. As the poet disappears in this way of writing, and does not deliver the intended censure in his own proper person, the satire becomes more delicate, because more oblique. Add to this, that a tale or story more strongly engages and interests the reader, than a series of precepts or reproofs, or even of characters themselves, however lively and natural. An heroi-comic poem may therefore be justly esteemed the most excellent kind of satire. . . .

The *Rape of the Lock,* now before us, is the . . . most excellent of the heroi-comic poems. . . .

[The] machines are vastly superior to the allegorical personages of Boileau and Garth; not only on account of their novelty, but for the exquisite poetry, and oblique satire, which they have given the poet an opportunity to display. . . .

The description of the toilette . . . is judiciously given in such magnificent terms, as dignify the offices performed at it. Belinda dressing is painted in as pompous a manner, as Achilles arming. . . .

The sacrifice of the baron to implore success to his undertaking, is another instance of our poet's judgment, in heightening the subject. The succeeding scene of sailing upon the Thames is most gay and *riant;* and impresses the most pleasing pictures upon the imagination. Here too the machinery is again introduced with much propriety. Ariel summons his denizens of air; who are . . . painted with a rich exuberance of fancy. . . . Those who are fond of tracing images and sentiments to their source, may perhaps be inclined to think, that the hint of ascribing tasks and offices to such imaginary beings, is taken from the Fairies and the Ariel of Shakespeare: let the impartial critic determine, which has the superiority of fancy. . . . Yet it must be granted, that by the addition of the most delicate satire to the most lively fancy, Pope, in the following passage, has excelled any thing in Shakespeare, or perhaps in any other author.

Our humbler province is to tend the fair,
Not a less pleasing, though less glorious care;
To save the powder from too rough a gale,
Nor let th' imprison'd essences exhale;
To draw fresh colours from the vernal flow'rs;
To steal from rainbows, e'er they drop in show'rs,
A brighter wash; to curl their waving hairs,
Assist their blushes, and inspire their airs;
Nay oft, in dreams invention we bestow,
To change a flounce, or add a furbelow. . . .

Our poet still rises in the delicacy of his satire, where he employs, with the utmost judgment and elegance, all the implements and furniture of the toilette, as instruments of punishment to those spirits, who shall be careless of their charge: of punishment such as sylphs alone could undergo. . . . [Quotes II, 125–136.] If Virgil has merited such perpetual commendation for exalting his bees, by the majesty and magnificence of his diction, does not Pope deserve equal praises, for the pomp and lustre of his language, on so trivial a subject? . . .

The parodies are some of the most exquisite parts of this poem. That which follows from the "Dum juga montis aper," of Virgil, contains some of the most artful strokes of satire, and the most poignant ridicule imaginable.

While fish in streams, or birds delight in air,
Or in a coach and six the British fair,

As long as Atalantis shall be read,
Or the small pillow grace a lady's bed,
While visits shall be paid on solemn days,
When numerous wax-lights in bright order blaze,
While nymphs take treats, or assignations give,
So long my honour, name and praise, shall live. . . .

Pope's parodies of the speech of Sarpedon in Homer, and of the description of Achilles's scepter, together with the scales of Jupiter from Homer, Virgil, and Milton, are judiciously introduced in their several places; are perhaps superiour to those Boileau or Garth have used, and are worked up with peculiar pleasantry. The mind of the reader is engaged by novelty, when it so unexpectedly finds a thought or object it had been accustomed to survey in another form, suddenly arrayed in a ridiculous garb. A mixture of comic and ridiculous images, with serious and important ones, is also no small beauty to this species of poetry. As in the following passages, where real and imaginary distresses are coupled together.

Not youthful kings in battle seiz'd alive,
Not scornful virgins who their charms survive,
Not ardent lovers robb'd of all their bliss,
Not ancient ladies when refus'd a kiss,
Not tyrants fierce that unrepenting die,

Nay, to carry the climax still higher,

Not Cynthia when her manteau's pinn'd awry,
E'er felt such rage resentment and despair. . . .

Upon the whole, I hope it will not be thought an exaggerated panegyric to say, that the *Rape of the Lock,* is the *best satire* extant; that it contains the truest and liveliest picture of modern life; and that the subject is of a more elegant nature, as well as more artfully conducted, than that of any other heroi-comic poem. . . .

It is in this composition, Pope principally appears a *poet;* in which he has displayed more imagination than in all his other works taken together. . . .

The *Elegy to the Memory of an Unfor-*

tunate Lady, . . . as it came from the heart, is very tender and pathetic; more so, I think, than any other copy of verses of our author. . . .

If this Elegy be so excellent, it may be ascribed to this cause; that the occasion of it was real; for it is certainly an indisputable maxim, "That nature is more powerful than fancy; that we can always feel more than we can imagine; and that the most artful fiction must give way to truth.". . .

The versification of [*Sappho to Phaon*] . . . is, in point of melody, next to that of his pastorals. Perhaps the two following lines, in which alliteration is successfully used, are the most harmonious verses in our language, I mean in rhyme:

Ye gentle gales! beneath my body blow,
And softly lay me on the waves below! . . .

No part of this poem [*Eloisa to Abelard*], or indeed of any of Pope's productions is so truly poetical, and contains such strong painting, as the passage to which we are now arrived;—the description of the convent, where Pope's religion certainly aided his fansy. It is impossible to read it without being struck with a pensive pleasure, and a sacred awe, at the solemnity of the scene; so picturesque are the epithets.

In these *lone* walls, (their days eternal bound)
These *moss-grown* domes with *spiry* turrets crown'd,
Where *awful* arches make the noonday night,
And the *dim* windows shed a *solemn* light;
Thy eyes diffus'd a reconciling ray.

All the circumstances that can amuse and sooth the mind of a solitary, are next enumerated in this expressive manner: and the reader that shall be disgusted at the length of the quotation, one might pronounce, has no taste, either for painting or poetry:

The darksome pines that o'er yon rocks reclin'd
Wave high, and murmur to the hollow wind,

The wand'ring streams that shine between the hills,
The grots that echo to the tinkling rills,
The dying gales that pant upon the trees,
The lakes that quiver to the curling breeze;
No more these scenes my meditation aid,
Or lull to rest the visionary maid.

The effect and influence of Melancholy, who is beautifully personified, on every object that occurs, and on every part of the convent, cannot be too much applauded, or too often read, as it is founded on nature and experience. That temper of mind casts a gloom on all things.

But o'er the twilight groves and dusky caves,
Long-sounding iles, and intermingled graves,
Black Melancholy sits, and round her throws
A death-like silence, and a dread repose;
Her gloomy presence saddens all the scene,
Shades every flower, and darkens every green,
Deepens the murmur of the falling floods,
And breathes a browner horror on the woods.

The figurative expressions, *throws*, and *breathes*, and *browner* horror, are, I verily believe, some of the strongest and boldest in the English language. The *image* of the Goddess Melancholy sitting over the convent, and as it were expanding her dreadful wings over its whole circuit, and diffusing her gloom all around it, is truly sublime, and strongly conceived. . . .

This Epistle, is, on the whole, one of the most highly finished, and certainly the most interesting, of the pieces of our author; and, together with the *Elegy to the Memory of an Unfortunate Lady*, is the only instance of the Pathetic Pope has given us. I think one may venture to remark, that the reputation of Pope, as a poet, among posterity, will be principally owing to his *Windsor-Forest*, his *Rape of the Lock*, and his *Eloisa to Abelard*: whilst the facts and characters alluded to and exposed, in his later writings, will be forgotten and unknown, and their poignancy and propriety little relished. For *wit* and *satire* are transitory and perishable, but *nature* and *passion* are eternal. . . .

The *Essay on Man* is as close a piece of argument, admitting its principles, as perhaps can be found in verse. Pope informs us in his *first* preface, "that he chose this epistolary way of writing, notwithstanding his subject was high, and of dignity, because of its being mixed with argument which of its nature approacheth to prose." He has not wandered into any useless digressions, has employed no fictions, no tale or story, and has relied chiefly on the poetry of his stile, for the purpose of interesting his readers. His stile is concise and figurative, forcible and elegant. He has many metaphors and images, artfully interspersed in the driest passages, which stood most in need of such ornaments. Nevertheless there are too many lines, in this performance, plain and prosaic. The meaner the subject is of a preceptive poem, the more striking appears the art of the poet: It is even of use to chuse a low subject. In this respect Virgil had the advantage over Lucretius; the latter with all his vigour and sublimity of genius, could hardly satisfy and come up to the grandeur of his theme. Pope labours under the same case. If any beauty in this Essay be uncommonly transcendent and peculiar, it is, *brevity of diction;* which, in a few instances, and those pardonable, have occasioned obscurity. It is hardly to be imagined how much sense, how much thinking, how much observation on human life, is condensed together in a small compass. . . .

[The] opening is awful, and commands the attention of the reader. The word *awake* has peculiar force, and obliquely alludes to his noble friend's leaving his political, for philosophical pursuits. May I venture to observe, that the metaphors in the succeeding lines, drawn from the field sports of setting and shooting, seem below the dignity of the subject; especially,

> *Eye* nature's walks, *shoot* folly as it flies,
> And *catch* the manners living as they *rise*. . . .

> The lamb thy riot dooms to bleed to day,
> Had he thy reason, would he skip and play?

> Pleas'd to the last, he crops the flowery food,
> And licks the hand just rais'd to shed his blood.

The tenderness of this striking image, and particularly the circumstance in the last line, has an artful effect in alleviating the dryness in the argumentative parts of the Essay, and interesting the reader. . . .

[Quotes I, 99–112.] Pope has indulged himself in but few digressions in this piece; this is one of the most poetical. Representations of undisguised nature and artless innocence always amuse and delight. The simple notions which uncivilized nations entertain of a future state, are many of them beautifully romantic, and some of the best subjects for poetry. It has been questioned whether the circumstance of the dog, although striking at the first view, is introduced with propriety, as it is known that the animal is not a native of America. The notion of seeing God in clouds, and hearing him in the wind, cannot be enough applauded.

> From burning suns when livid deaths descend,
> When earthquakes swallow, or when tempests sweep
> Towns to one grave, whole nations to the deep.

I quote these lines as an example of energy of stile, and of Pope's manner of compressing together many images, without confusion, and without superfluous epithets. Substantives and verbs are the sinews of language. . . .

> From the *green* myriads in the *peopled* grass—
> The mole's *dim* curtain, and the lynx's beam;
> Of smell the *headlong* lioness between,
> And hound sagacious on the *tainted* green:
> The spider's touch how exquisitely fine,
> Feels at each thread, and lives along the line.

These lines are selected as admirable patterns of forcible diction. The peculiar and discriminating expressiveness of the epithets distinguished above by italics will be particularly regarded. Perhaps we have no image in the language, more lively than that of the last verse. "To live along the line" is equally bold and beautiful. In this part of this Epistle the poet seems to have remarkably laboured his style, which abounds in various figures, and is much elevated. Pope has practised the great secret of Virgil's art, which was to discover the very single epithet that precisely suited each occasion. . . .

[Quotes I, 267–280.] Whilst I am transcribing this exalted description of the omnipresence of the Deity, I feel myself almost tempted to retract an assertion in the beginning of this work, that there is nothing transcendently sublime in Pope. These lines have all the energy and harmony that can be given to rhyme. . . .

> Who taught the nations of the field and wood
> To shun their poison, and to chuse their food?
> Prescient, the tides or tempests to withstand,
> Build on the wave, or arch beneath the sand?

This passage is highly finished; such objects are more suited to the nature of poetry than abstract ideas. Every verb and epithet has here a descriptive force. We find more imagery from these lines to the end of the epistle, than in any other parts of this Essay. . . .

> He from the wond'ring furrow call'd the food,
> Taught to command the fire, controul the flood,
> Draw forth the monsters of th' abyss profound,
> Or fetch the aerial eagle to the ground.

A finer example can perhaps scarce be given of a compact and comprehensive stile. The manner in which the four elements were subdued is comprised in these four lines alone. Pope is here, as Quintilian says of another, densus et brevis et instans sibi. There is not an useless word in this passage; there are but three epithets, *wondering, profound, aerial*; and they are placed precisely with the very substantive that is of most consequence: if there had been epithets joined with the other substantives, it would have weakened the nervousness of the sentence. This was a secret of versification Pope well understood, and hath often practised with peculiar success. . . .

> ————A better wou'd you fix?
> Then give Humility a coach and six.

> Worth makes the man, and want of it the fellow;
> The rest is all but leather or prunella.

> Not one looks backward, onward still he goes,
> Yet ne'er looks forward further than his nose.

> To sigh for ribbands if thou art so silly,
> Mark how they grace Lord Umbra or Sir Billy.

In a work of so serious and severe a cast, in a work of reasoning, in a work of theology designed to explain the most interesting subject that can employ the mind of man, surely such strokes of levity, of satire, of ridicule, however poignant and witty, are ill placed and disgusting, are violations of that propriety which Pope in general so strictly observed. . . .

> Narcissa's nature, tolerably mild,
> To make a wash, would hardly stew a child;
> Has ev'n been prov'd to grant a lover's pray'r;
> And paid a tradesman once to make him stare;
> Gave alms at Easter, in a Christian trim,
> And made a widow happy for a whim.

The epistle on the characters of women, from whence this truly witty character is taken, is highly finished, and full of the most delicate satire. Bolingbroke, a judge of the subject, thought it the master-piece of Pope. Pleasantry reigns throughout it; and the bitterness of the satire is concealed in a laugh. The characters are lively, though uncommon. I scarcely remember one of them in our comic writers of the best order. The ridicule is heightened by many such strokes of humour, carried even to the borders of extravagance, as that in the second line, here quoted. . . .

> See how the world its veterans rewards,
> A youth of frolics, an old age of cards;
> Fair to no purpose, artful to no end,
> Young without lovers, old without a friend;
> A fop their passion, but their prize a sot,
> Alive, ridiculous; and dead, forgot.

The antithesis, so remarkably strong in these lines, was a very favourite figure with our poet: he has indeed used it but in too many parts of his works; nay, even in his translation of the Iliad; where it ought not to have been admitted. Our author seldom writes many lines together without an antithesis. It must be allowed sometimes to add strength to a sentiment, by an opposition of images; but, too frequently repeated, it becomes tiresome, and disgusting. . . .

Kept dross for Duchesses, *the world shall know it*,
To you gave sense, good-humour, and a poet.

The world shall know it—is a bad expression, and a poor expletive, into which our poet was forced by the rhyme. . . .
Rhyme also could alone be the occasion of the following faulty expressions; taken too from some of his most finished pieces.

Not Caesar's Empress would *I deign to prove*—
If Queenberry to strip *there's no compelling*—
Wrapt into future times the *bard begun*—
Know all the noise the busy *world can keep*—
If true, a woful likeness, and *if lyes*—
Nothing so true as what you once *let fall*—
For virtue's self may too much *zeal be bad*—
———————— can no *wants endure*—
Nay half in heav'n *except what's mighty odd*—
———————— listening ears *employ*—
———————— on such a world *we fall*—
———————— take scandal *at a spark*—
———————— do *the knack*, and ————————
do *the feat*.—

And more instances might be added, if it were not disagreeable to observe these straws in amber. But if rhyme occasions such inconveniences and improprieties in so exact a writer as our author, what can be expected from inferior versifiers? It is not my intention to enter into a trite and tedious discussion of the several merits of rhyme and blank verse. Perhaps rhyme may be properest for shorter pieces; for didactic, lyric, elegiac, and satiric poems; for pieces where closeness of expression, and smartness of style, are expected; but for

subjects of a higher order, or for poems of a greater length, blank verse may be preferable. An epic poem in rhyme appears to be such a sort of thing, as the Aeneid would have been if it had been written, like Ovid's Fasti, in hexameter and pentameter verses; and the reading it would have been as tedious as the travelling through that one, long, strait, avenue of firs, that leads from Moscow to Petersburg. . . .
"Not one of my works" (said Pope to Mr. Spence) "was more laboured than my epistle on the Use of Riches." It does indeed abound in knowledge of life, and in the justest satire. . . . And tho' it was difficult to say any thing new about avarice, "a vice that has been so pelted" (says Cowley) "with good sentences," yet has our author done it so successfully, that this epistle, together with Lord Bacon's thirty-third *Essay*, contains almost all that can be said on the use and abuse of riches, and the absurd extremes of avarice and profusion. But our poet has enlivened his precepts with so many various characters, pictures, and images, as may entitle him to claim the preference over all that have treated on this tempting subject, down from the time of the Plutus of Aristophanes. . . .
[Quotes Epistle III, lines 187–196, 299–305.] The use, the force, and the excellence of language, certainly consists in raising *clear, complete,* and *circumstantial* images, and in turning *readers* into *spectators.* I have quoted the two preceding passages as eminent examples of this excellence, of all others the most essential in poetry. Every epithet, here used, *paints* its object, and *paints* it *distinctly.* After having passed over the moat full of cresses, do you not *actually* find yourself in the middle court of this forlorn and solitary mansion, overgrown with docks and nettles? And do you not hear the dog that is going to assault you? . . .

Who shames a scribbler? break one cobweb thro',
He spins the slight, self-pleasing thread anew:
Destroy his fib or sophistry, in vain!

The creature's at his dirty work again;
Thron'd in the center of his thin designs,
Proud of a vast extent of flimsy lines.
    [*Epistle to Dr. Arbuthnot,* lines 89–94]

The *metaphor* is most happily carried on through a variety of corresponding particulars, that exactly hit the natures of the two *insects* in question. It is not pursued *too far,* nor jaded out, so as to become *quaint* and *affected,* as is the case of many, perhaps, in Congreve's Comedies, particularly in the Way of the World, and in Young's Satires. . . .

Yet then did Gildon draw his venal quill;
I wish'd the man a dinner, and sat still:
Yet then did Dennis rave in furious fret;
I never answer'd, I was not in debt:
If want provok'd, or madness made them print,
I wag'd no war with Bedlam or the Mint.

The unexpected turn in the second line of each of these three couplets, contains as cutting and bitter strokes of satire, as perhaps can be written. . . .

The famous character of Atticus . . . is perhaps the finest piece of satire extant.[1] . . .

[Quotes lines 305–333, on Sporus.] Language cannot afford more glowing or more forcible terms to express the utmost bitterness of contempt. We think we are here reading Milton against Salmasius. The raillery is carried to the very verge of *railing,* some will say *ribaldry.* He has armed his muse with a scalping-knife. The portrait is certainly *over-charged.* . . .

That not in Fancy's maze he wander'd long,
But stoop'd to *Truth,* and moraliz'd his song.

Here is our author's own declaration, delivered in the most precise and positive terms, that he early left the *more poetical* provinces of his art, to become a moral, didactic, and satiric poet. . . .

[Quotes lines 406–413.] These exquisite lines give us a very interesting picture of

[1] This sentence is inserted here from Vol. I, p. 156.

the exemplary filial piety of our author. There is a pensive and pathetic sweetness in the very flow of them. The eye that has been wearied and opprest by the harsh and austere colouring of some of the preceding passages, turns away with pleasure from these asperities, and reposes with complacency on the soft tints of domestic tenderness. We are naturally gratified to see great men descending from their heights, into the familiar offices of common life; and the sensation is the more pleasing to us, because *admiration* is turned into *affection.* . . .

No part of our author's works have been more admired than these imitations [of Horace]. The aptness of the allusions, and the happiness of many of the parallels, give a pleasure that is always no small one to the mind of a reader, the pleasure of *comparison.* He that has the least acquaintance with these pieces of Horace, which resemble the Old Comedy, immediately perceives, indeed, that our author has assumed a higher tone, and frequently has deserted the free colloquial air, the insinuating Socratic manner of his original. And that he clearly resembles in his style, as he did in his natural temper, the severe and serious Juvenal, more than the smiling and sportive Horace. . . .

[Of the *Dunciad,* 1729:] Thus far all was clear, consistent, and of a piece; and was delivered in such nervous and spirited versification, that the delighted reader had only to lament that so many poetical beauties were thrown away on such dirty and despicable subjects, as were the scribblers here proscribed; who appear like monsters preserved in the most costly *spirits.* But in the year 1742, our poet was persuaded, unhappily enough, to add a *fourth* book to his *finished* piece, of such a very different cast and colour, as to render it at last one of the most motley compositions, that perhaps is any where to be found, in the works of so exact a writer as Pope. For one great purpose of this *fourth* book, (where, by the way, the hero does nothing at all) was to satirize and proscribe infidels, and free-thinkers, to leave the ludicrous for the serious, Grub-street for theology, the mock-heroic for metaphysics; which occasioned a marvellous mixture and jumble of images and sentiments, Pantomime and Philosophy, Journals and Moral evidence, Fleet-ditch and the High Priori road, Curl and Clarke.—To ridicule our fashionable libertines, and affected minute philosophers, was doubtless a most laudable intention; but speaking of the Dunciad as a work of art, in a critical not a religious light, we must venture to affirm, that the subject of this fourth book was foreign and heterogeneous, and the addition of it as injudicious, ill-placed, and incongruous, as any of those dissimilar images we meet with in Pulci or Ariosto. It is like introducing a crucifix into one of Teniers's burlesque conversation-pieces. Some of his most splendid and striking lines are indeed here to be found; but we must beg leave to insist that they want *propriety* and *decorum,* and must wish they had adorned some *separate* work, against irreligion, which would have been worthy the pen of our bitter and immortal satirist. . . .

The chief fault of the Dunciad is the *violence and vehemence of its satire, and the excessive heighth to which it is carried; and

* Which sour the temper of the reader; insomuch that I know a person, whose name would be an ornament to these papers, if I was suffered to insert it, who, after reading a book of the Dunciad, always *sooths* himself, as he calls it, by turning to a canto in the Fairy Queen. This is not the case in that very delightful and beautiful poem, *Mac Flecnoe,* from which Pope has borrowed so many hints, and images, and ideas. But Dryden's poem was the offspring of *contempt,* and Pope's of *indignation:* one is full of *mirth,* and the other of *malignity.* A vein of pleasantry is uniformly preserved through the whole of Mac Flecnoe, and the piece begins and ends in the *same key.* It is natural and obvious to borrow a metaphor from music, when we are speaking of a poem whose versification is particularly and exquisitely sweet and harmonious. The numbers of the Dunciad, by being much laboured, and encumbered with epithets, have something in them of stiffness and harshness. . . . .

which therefore I have heard compared to that marvellous column of boiling water, near mount Hecla, thrown upwards, above ninety feet, by the force of a subterraneous fire. . . .

[The epitaphs] are all in general overrun with point and antithesis, and are a kind of panegyrical epigrams. They are, consequently, very different from the *simple sepulchral* inscriptions of the ancients. . . .

Thus have we endeavoured to give a critical account, with freedom, but it is hoped with impartiality, of each of Pope's works; by which review it will appear, that the *largest* portion of them is of the *didactic, moral,* and *satyric* kind; and consequently, not of the most *poetic* species of *poetry;* whence it is manifest, that *good sense* and *judgment* were his characteristical excellencies, rather than *fancy* and *invention;* not that the author of the *Rape of the Lock,* and *Eloisa,* can be thought to want *imagination,* but because his *imagination* was not his predominant talent, because he indulged it not, and because he gave not so many proofs of *this* talent as of the *other.* . . . He gradually became one of the most correct, even, and exact poets that ever wrote; polishing his pieces with a care and assiduity, that no business or avocation ever interrupted: so that if he does not frequently ravish and transport his reader, yet he does not disgust him with unexpected inequalities, and absurd improprieties. Whatever poetical enthusiasm he actually possessed, he withheld and stifled. The perusal of him affects not our minds with such strong emotions as we feel from Homer and Milton; so that no man of a true poetical spirit, *is master of himself while he reads* them. Hence, he is a writer fit for universal perusal; adapted to all ages and stations; for the old and for the young; the man of business and the scholar. He who would think *Palamon and Arcite,* the *Tempest* or *Comus,* childish and romantic, might relish Pope. Surely it is no narrow and niggardly encomium to say he is the great Poet of Reason, the *first* of *ethical* authors in verse. And this species of writing is, after all, the surest road to an extensive reputation. It lies more level to the general capacities of men, than the higher flights of more genuine poetry. . . .

Where then, . . . shall we with justice be authorized to place our admired Pope? Not, assuredly, in the same rank with Spencer, Shakespeare, and Milton; however justly we may applaud the *Eloisa* and *Rape* of the Lock; but, considering the correctness, elegance, and utility of his works, the weight of sentiment, and the knowledge of man they contain, we may venture to assign him a place, *next* to Milton, and *just* above Dryden. Yet, to bring our minds steadily to make this decision, we must forget, for a moment, the divine *Music Ode* of Dryden; and may perhaps then be compelled to confess, that though Dryden be the greater genius, yet Pope is the better artist.

Samuel Johnson

Alexander Pope

OF HIS intellectual character, the constituent and fundamental principle was good sense, a prompt and intuitive perception of consonance and propriety. He saw immediately, of his own conceptions, what was to be chosen, and what to be rejected; and, in the works of others, what was to be shunned, and what was to be copied.

But good sense alone is a sedate and quiescent quality, which manages its possessions well, but does not increase them; it collects few materials for its own operations, and preserves safety, but never gains supremacy. Pope had likewise genius; a mind active, ambitious, and adventurous, always investigating, always aspiring; in its widest searches still longing to go forward, in its highest flights still wishing to be higher; always imagining something greater than it knows, always endeavouring more than it can do.

To assist these powers, he is said to have had great strength and exactness of memory. That which he had heard or read was not easily lost; and he had before him not only what his own meditations suggested, but what he had found in other writers, that might be accommodated to his present purpose.

These benefits of nature he improved by incessant and unwearied diligence; he had recourse to every source of intelligence, and lost no opportunity of information; he consulted the living as well as the dead; he read his compositions to his friends, and was never content with mediocrity when excellence could be attained. He considered poetry as the business of his life; and,

however he might seem to lament his occupation, he followed it with constancy; to make verses was his first labour, and to mend them was his last. . . .

The Works of Pope are now to be distinctly examined, not so much with attention to slight faults or petty beauties, as to the general character and effect of each performance.

It seems natural for a young poet to initiate himself by pastorals, which, not professing to imitate real life, require no experience; and, exhibiting only the simple operation of unmingled passions, admit no subtle reasoning or deep inquiry. Pope's *Pastorals* are not, however, composed but with close thought; they have reference to the time of the day, the seasons of the year, and the periods of human life. The last, that which turns the attention upon age and death, was the author's favourite. To tell of disappointment and misery, to thicken the darkness of futurity, and perplex the labyrinth of uncertainty, has been always a delicious employment of the poets. His preference was probably just. I wish, however, that his fondness had not overlooked a line in which the *Zephyrs* are made *to lament in silence*. To charge these *Pastorals* with want of invention, is to require what was never intended. The imitations are so ambitiously frequent, that the writer evidently means rather to show his literature than his wit. It is surely sufficient for an author of sixteen, not only to be able to copy the poems of antiquity with judicious selection, but to have obtained sufficient power of language and skill in metre to exhibit a se-

From *Lives of the English Poets* (1779–81); reprinted from the Everyman's Library edition, 2 vols., London, J. M. Dent & Sons Ltd., 1953, II, 143–243. (Bracketed passages below are inserted from the biographical part of the *Life*.)

ries of versification which had in English poetry no precedent, nor has since had an imitation.

The design of *Windsor Forest* is evidently derived from *Cooper's Hill*, with some attention to Waller's poem on *The Park;* but Pope cannot be denied to excel his masters in variety and elegance, and the art of interchanging description, narrative, and morality. The objection made by Dennis is the want of plan, of a regular subordination of parts terminating in the principal and original design. There is this want in most descriptive poems, because as the scenes, which they must exhibit successively, are all subsisting at the same time, the order in which they are shown must by necessity be arbitrary, and more is not to be expected from the last part than from the first. The attention, therefore, which cannot be detained by suspense, must be excited by diversity, such as his poem offers to its reader.

But the desire of diversity may be too much indulged; the parts of *Windsor Forest* which deserve least praise, are those which were added to enliven the stillness of the scene, the appearance of Father Thames, and the transformation of Lodona. Addison had in his *Campaign* derided the rivers that "rise from their oozy beds" to tell stories of heroes; and it is therefore strange that Pope should adopt a fiction not only unnatural, but lately censured. The story of Lodona is told with sweetness; but a new metamorphosis is a ready and puerile expedient: nothing is easier than to tell how a flower was once a blooming virgin, or a rock an obdurate tyrant.

The *Temple of Fame* has, as Steele warmly declared, "a thousand beauties." Every part is splendid; there is great luxuriance of ornaments; the original vision of Chaucer was never denied to be much improved; the allegory is very skilfully continued, the imagery is properly selected, and learnedly displayed: yet, with all this comprehension of excellence, as its scene is laid in remote ages, and its sentiments, if

the concluding paragraph be excepted, have little relation to general manners or common life, it never obtained much notice, but is turned silently over, and seldom quoted or mentioned with either praise or blame.

That the *Messiah* excels the *Pollio* is no great praise, if it be considered from what original the improvements are derived.

The *Verses on the Unfortunate Lady* have drawn much attention by the illaudable singularity of treating suicide with respect; and they must be allowed to be written in some parts with vigorous animation, and in others with gentle tenderness; nor has Pope produced any poem in which the sense predominates more over the diction. But the tale is not skilfully told; it is not easy to discover the character of either the Lady or her Guardian. History relates that she was about to disparage herself by a marriage with an inferior; Pope praises her for the dignity of ambition, and yet condemns the uncle to detestation for his pride; the ambitious love of a niece may be opposed by the interest, malice, or envy of an uncle, but never by his pride. On such an occasion a poet may be allowed to be obscure, but inconsistency never can be right. [Poetry has not often been worse employed than in dignifying the amorous fury of a raving girl.]

The *Ode for St. Cecilia's Day* was undertaken at the desire of Steele: in this the author is generally confessed to have miscarried, yet he has miscarried only as compared with Dryden; for he has far outgone other competitors. Dryden's plan is better chosen; history will always take stronger hold of the attention than fable: the passions excited by Dryden are the pleasures and pains of real life, the scene of Pope is laid in imaginary existence; Pope is read with calm acquiescence, Dryden with turbulent delight; Pope hangs upon the ear, and Dryden finds the passes of the mind. . . .

Poets do not always express their own thoughts: Pope, with all this labour in the praise of music, was ignorant of its principles, and insensible of its effects.

One of his greatest, though of his earliest works, is the *Essay on Criticism*, which, if he had written nothing else, would have placed him among the first critics and the first poets, as it exhibits every mode of excellence that can embellish or dignify didactic composition—selection of matter, novelty of arrangement, justness of precept, splendour of illustration, and propriety of digression. I know not whether it be pleasing to consider that he produced this piece at twenty, and never afterwards excelled it: he that delights himself with observing that such powers may be soon attained, cannot but grieve to think that life was ever after at a stand.

To mention the particular beauties of the *Essay* would be unprofitably tedious; but I cannot forbear to observe, that the comparison of a student's progress in the sciences with the journey of a traveller in the Alps, is perhaps the best that English poetry can show. A simile, to be perfect, must both illustrate and ennoble the subject; must show it to the understanding in a clearer view, and display it to the fancy with greater dignity; but either of these qualities may be sufficient to recommend it. In didactic poetry, of which the great purpose is instruction, a simile may be praised which illustrates, though it does not ennoble; in heroics, that may be admitted which ennobles, though it does not illustrate. That it may be complete, it is required to exhibit, independently of its references, a pleasing image; for a simile is said to be a short episode. To this antiquity was so attentive, that circumstances were sometimes added, which, having no parallels, served only to fill the imagination, and produced what Perrault ludicrously called "comparisons with a long tail." In their similes the greatest writers have sometimes failed: the ship-race, compared with the chariot-race, is neither illustrated nor aggrandised; land and water make all the difference: when Apollo, run-

ning after Daphne, is likened to a greyhound chasing a hare, there is nothing gained; the ideas of pursuit and flight are too plain to be made plainer; and a god and the daughter of a god are not represented much to their advantage by a hare and dog. The simile of the Alps has no useless parts, yet affords a striking picture by itself; it makes the foregoing position better understood, and enables it to take faster hold on the attention; it assists the apprehension and elevates the fancy.

Let me likewise dwell a little on the celebrated paragraph in which it is directed that "the sound should seem an echo to the sense"; a precept which Pope is allowed to have observed beyond any other English poet.

This notion of representative metre, and the desire of discovering frequent adaptations of the sound to the sense, have produced, in my opinion, many wild conceits and imaginary beauties. All that can furnish this representation are the sounds of the words considered singly, and the time in which they are pronounced. Every language has some words framed to exhibit the noises which they express, as *thump, rattle, growl, hiss*. These, however, are but few; and the poet cannot make them more, nor can they be of any use but when sound is to be mentioned. The time of pronunciation was in the dactylic measures of the learned languages capable of considerable variety; but that variety could be accommodated only to motion or duration, and different degrees of motion were perhaps expressed by verses rapid or slow, without much attention of the writer, when the image had full possession of his fancy; but our language having little flexibility, our verses can differ very little in their cadence. The fancied resemblances, I fear, arise sometimes merely from the ambiguity of words; there is supposed to be some relation between a *soft* line and *soft* couch, or between *hard* syllables and *hard* fortune.

Motion, however, may be in some sort exemplified; and yet it may be suspected that in such resemblances the mind often governs the ear, and the sounds are estimated by their meaning. One of their most successful attempts has been to describe the labour of Sisyphus:

With many a weary step, and many a groan,
Up the high hill he heaves a huge round stone;
The huge round stone, resulting with a bound,
Thunders impetuous down, and smokes along
   the ground.

Who does not perceive the stone to move slowly upward, and roll violently back? But set the same numbers to another sense:

While many a merry tale, and many a song,
Cheer'd the rough road, we wish'd the rough
   road long;
The rough road then, returning in a round,
Mock'd our impatient steps, for all was fairy
   ground.

We have now surely lost much of the delay, and much of the rapidity.

But, to show how little the greatest master of numbers can fix the principles of representative harmony, it will be sufficient to remark that the poet who tells us that

When Ajax strives some rock's vast weight to
   throw,
The line too labours, and the words move slow;
Not so when swift Camilla scours the plain,
Flies o'er th' unbending corn, and skims along
   the main;

when he had enjoyed for about thirty years the praise of Camilla's lightness of foot, he tried another experiment upon *sound* and *time,* and produced this memorable triplet:

Waller was smooth; but Dryden taught to join
The varying verse, the full resounding line,
The long majestic march, and energy divine.

Here are the swiftness of the rapid race, and the march of slow-paced majesty, exhibited by the same poet in the same sequence of syllables, except that the exact prosodist will find the line of *swiftness* by one time longer than that of *tardiness.*

Beauties of this kind are commonly fancied; and, when real, are technical and

nugatory, not to be rejected, and not to be solicited.

[Not long after he wrote *The Rape of the Lock,* the most airy, the most ingenious, and the most delightful of all his compositions. . . .

At its first appearance it was termed by Addison "merum sal." Pope, however, saw that it was capable of improvement; and having luckily contrived to borrow his machinery from the Rosicrucians, imparted the scheme with which his head was teeming to Addison, who told him that his work, as it stood, was "a delicious little thing," and gave him no encouragement to retouch it.

This has been too hastily considered as an instance of Addison's jealousy; for as he could not guess the conduct of the new design, or the possibilities of pleasure comprised in a fiction of which there had been no examples, he might very reasonably and kindly persuade the author to acquiesce in his own prosperity, and forbear an attempt which he considered as an unnecessary hazard.

Addison's counsel was happily rejected. Pope foresaw the future efflorescence of imagery then budding in his mind, and resolved to spare no art or industry of cultivation. The soft luxuriance of his fancy was already shooting, and all the gay varieties of diction were ready at his hand to colour and embellish it.

His attempt was justified by its success. *The Rape of the Lock* stands forward, in the classes of literature, as the most exquisite example of ludicrous poetry. Berkeley congratulated him upon the display of powers more truly poetical than he had shown before: with elegance of description and justness of precepts he had now exhibited boundless fertility of invention.

He always considered the intermixture of the machinery with the action as his most successful exertion of poetical art. He indeed could never afterwards produce anything of such unexampled excellence. Those performances which strike with wonder, are combinations of skilful genius with happy casualty; and it is not likely that any felicity, like the discovery of a new race of preternatural agents, should happen twice to the same man.]

. . . In this work are exhibited, in a very high degree, the two most engaging powers of an author. New things are made familiar, and familiar things are made new. A race of aerial people, never heard of before, is presented to us in a manner so clear and easy, that the reader seeks for no further information, but immediately mingles with his new acquaintance, adopts their interests, and attends their pursuits, loves a sylph, and detests a gnome.

That familiar things are made new, every paragraph will prove. The subject of the poem is an event below the common incidents of common life; nothing real is introduced that is not seen so often as to be no longer regarded; yet the whole detail of a female-day is here brought before us, invested with so much art of decoration, that, though nothing is disguised, everything is striking, and we feel all the appetite of curiosity for that from which we have a thousand times turned fastidiously away.

The purpose of the poet is, as he tells us, to laugh at "the little unguarded follies of the female sex." It is therefore without justice that Dennis charges *The Rape of the Lock* with the want of a moral, and for that reason sets it below the *Lutrin,* which exposes the pride and discord of the clergy. Perhaps neither Pope nor Boileau has made the world much better than he found it; but, if they had both succeeded, it were easy to tell who would have deserved most from public gratitude. The freaks, and humours, and spleen, and vanity of women, as they embroil families in discord, and fill houses with disquiet, do more to obstruct the happiness of life in a year than the ambition of the clergy in many centuries. It has been well observed, that the misery of man proceeds not from any single crush of overwhelming evil, but from small vexations continually repeated.

It is remarked by Dennis likewise that the machinery is superfluous; that, by all the bustle of preternatural operation, the main event is neither hastened nor retarded. To this charge an efficacious answer is not easily made. The Sylphs cannot be said to help or to oppose, and it must be allowed to imply some want of art, that their power has not been sufficiently intermingled with the action. Other parts may likewise be charged with want of connection; the game at *ombre* might be spared; but if the Lady had lost her hair while she was intent upon her cards, it might have been inferred that those who are too fond of play will be in danger of neglecting more important interests. Those perhaps are faults; but what are such faults to so much excellence?

The Epistle of Eloisa to Abelard is one of the most happy productions of human wit; the subject is so judiciously chosen, that it would be difficult, in turning over the annals of the world, to find another which so many circumstances concur to recommend. We regularly interest ourselves most in the fortune of those who most deserve our notice. Abelard and Eloisa were conspicuous in their days for eminence of merit. The heart naturally loves truth. The adventures and misfortunes of this illustrious pair are known from undisputed history. Their fate does not leave the mind in hopeless dejection, for they both found quiet and consolation in retirement and piety. So new and so affecting is their story, that it supersedes invention, and imagination ranges at full liberty without straggling into scenes of fable.

The story, thus skilfully adopted, has been diligently improved. Pope has left nothing behind him which seems more the effect of studious perseverance and laborious revisal. Here is particularly observable the *curiosa felicitas,* a fruitful soil and careful cultivation. Here is no crudeness of sense, nor asperity of language. . . .

The train of my disquisition has now conducted me to that poetical wonder, the translation of the Iliad, a performance which no age or nation can pretend to equal. . . .

The chief help of Pope in this arduous undertaking was drawn from the versions of Dryden. Virgil had borrowed much of his imagery from Homer, and part of the debt was now paid by his translator. Pope searched the pages of Dryden for happy combinations of heroic diction; but it will not be denied that he added much to what he found. He cultivated our language with so much diligence and art that he has left in his Homer a treasure of poetical elegances to posterity. His version may be said to have tuned the English tongue; for since its appearance no writer, however deficient in other powers, has wanted melody. Such a series of lines, so elaborately corrected and so sweetly modulated, took possession of the public ear; the vulgar was enamoured of the poem, and the learned wondered at the translation.

But in the most general applause discordant voices will always be heard. It has been objected by some, who wish to be numbered among the sons of learning, that Pope's version of Homer is not Homerical; that it exhibits no resemblance of the original and characteristic manner of the father of poetry, as it wants his awful simplicity, his artless grandeur, his unaffected majesty. This cannot be totally denied; but it must be remembered that *necessitas quod cogit defendit;* that may be lawfully done which cannot be forborne. Time and place will always enforce regard. In estimating this translation, consideration must be had of the nature of our language, the form of our metre, and above all of the change which two thousand years have made in the modes of life and the habits of thought. Virgil wrote in a language of the same general fabric with that of Homer, in verses of the same measure, and in an age nearer to Homer's time by eighteen hundred years, yet he found, even then, the state of the world so much altered, and the demand for elegance so much increased, that mere nature would be endured no longer; and

perhaps, in the multitude of borrowed passages, very few can be shown which he has not embellished.

There is a time when nations emerging from barbarity, and falling into regular subordination, gain leisure to grow wise, and feel the shame of ignorance and the craving pain of unsatisfied curiosity. To this hunger of the mind plain sense is grateful; that which fills the void removes uneasiness, and to be free from pain for a while is pleasure; but repletion generates fastidiousness; a saturated intellect soon becomes luxurious, and knowledge finds no willing reception till it is recommended by artificial diction. Thus it will be found, in the progress of learning, that in all nations the first writers are simple, and that every age improves in elegance. One refinement always makes way for another; and what was expedient to Virgil was necessary to Pope.

I suppose many readers of the English Iliad, when they have been touched with some unexpected beauty of the lighter kind, have tried to enjoy it in the original, where, alas! it was not to be found. Homer doubtless owes to his translator many Ovidian graces not exactly suitable to his character; but to have added can be no great crime, if nothing be taken away. Elegance is surely to be desired, if it be not gained at the expense of dignity. A hero would wish to be loved as well as to be reverenced.

To a thousand cavils one answer is sufficient: the purpose of a writer is to be read, and the criticism which would destroy the power of pleasing must be blown aside. Pope wrote for his own age and his own nation; he knew that it was necessary to colour the images and point the sentiments of his author; he therefore made him graceful, but lost him some of his sublimity. . . .

Of *The Dunciad* the hint is confessedly taken from Dryden's *Mac Flecknoe;* but the plan is so enlarged and diversified as justly to claim the praise of an original, and affords perhaps the best specimen that has yet appeared of personal satire ludicrously pompous.

That the design was moral, whatever the author might tell either his readers or himself, I am not convinced. The first motive was the desire of revenging the contempt with which Theobald had treated his Shakespeare, and regaining the honour which he had lost, by crushing his opponent. Theobald was not of bulk enough to fill a poem, and therefore it was necessary to find other enemies with other names, at whose expense he might divert the public.

In this design there was petulance and malignity enough; but I cannot think it very criminal. An author places himself uncalled before the tribunal of criticism, and solicits fame at the hazard of disgrace. Dullness or deformity are not culpable in themselves, but may be very justly reproached when they pretend to the honour of wit or the influence of beauty. If bad writers were to pass without reprehension, what should restrain them? *impune diem consumpserit ingens Telephus;* and upon bad writers only will censure have much effect. The satire which brought Theobald and Moore into contempt, dropped impotent from Bentley like the javelin of Priam.

All truth is valuable, and satirical criticism may be considered as useful when it rectifies error and improves judgment; he that refines the public taste is a public benefactor.

The beauties of this poem are well known; its chief fault is the grossness of its images. Pope and Swift had an unnatural delight in ideas physically impure, such as every other tongue utters with unwillingness, and of which every ear shrinks from the mention.

But even this fault, offensive as it is, may be forgiven for the excellence of other passages—such as the formation and dissolution of Moore, the account of the Traveller, the misfortune of the Florist, and the crowded thoughts and stately numbers which dignify the concluding paragraph.

. . . [He published (October 1743) a new edition of *The Dunciad,* in which he degraded Theobald from his painful preeminence, and enthroned Cibber in his stead. Unhappily the two heroes were of opposite characters, and Pope was unwilling to lose what he had already written; he has therefore depraved his poem by giving to Cibber the old books, the cold pedantry, and sluggish pertinacity of Theobald.]

The Essay on Man was a work of great labour and long consideration, but certainly not the happiest of Pope's performances. The subject is perhaps not very proper for poetry, and the poet was not sufficiently master of his subject; metaphysical morality was to him a new study, he was proud of his acquisitions, and, supposing himself master of great secrets, was in haste to teach what he had not learned. Thus he tells us, in the first epistle, that from the nature of the Supreme Being may be deduced an order of beings such as mankind, because Infinite Excellence can do only what is best. He finds out that these beings must be "somewhere," and that "all the question is whether man be in a wrong place." Surely if, according to the poet's Leibnitian reasoning, we may infer that man ought to be, only because he is, we may allow that his place is the right place because he has it. Supreme Wisdom is not less infallible in disposing than in creating. But what is meant by *somewhere* and *place,* and *wrong place,* it had been vain to ask Pope, who probably had never asked himself.

Having exalted himself into the chair of wisdom, he tells us much that every man knows, and much that he does not know himself: that we see but little, and that the order of the universe is beyond our comprehension—an opinion not very uncommon; and that there is a chain of subordinate beings "from infinite to nothing," of which himself and his readers are equally ignorant. But he gives us one comfort which, without his help, he supposes unattainable, in the position "that though we are fools, yet God is wise."

This essay affords an egregious instance of the predominance of genius, the dazzling splendour of imagery, and the seductive powers of eloquence. Never was penury of knowledge and vulgarity of sentiment so happily disguised. The reader feels his mind full, though he learns nothing; and when he meets it in its new array, no longer knows the talk of his mother and his nurse. When these wonder-working sounds sink into sense, and the doctrine of the *Essay,* disrobed of its ornaments, is left to the powers of its naked excellence, what shall we discover? That we are, in comparison with our Creator, very weak and ignorant—that we do not uphold the chain of existence—and that we could not make one another with more skill than we are made. We may learn yet more—that the arts of human life were copied from the instinctive operations of other animals—that if the world be made for man, it may be said that man was made for geese. To these profound principles of natural knowledge are added some moral instructions equally new: that self-interest, well understood, will produce social concord—that men are mutual gainers by mutual benefits—that evil is sometimes balanced by good—that human advantages are unstable and fallacious, of uncertain duration and doubtful effect—that our true honour is, not to have a great part, but to act it well—that virtue only is our own—and that happiness is always in our power.

Surely a man of no very comprehensive search may venture to say that he has heard all this before; but it was never till now recommended by such a blaze of embellishments, or such sweetness of melody. The vigorous contraction of some thoughts, the luxuriant amplification of others, the incidental illustrations, and sometimes the dignity, sometimes the softness of the verses, enchain philosophy, suspend criticism, and oppress judgment by overpowering pleasure.

This is true of many paragraphs; yet if I had undertaken to exemplify Pope's felicity of composition before a rigid critic, I should not select the *Essay on Man;* for it contains more lines unsuccessfully laboured, more harshness of diction, more thoughts imperfectly expressed, more levity without elegance, and more heaviness without strength, than will easily be found in all his other works.

The *Characters of Men and Women* are the product of diligent speculation upon human life; much labour has been bestowed upon them, and Pope very seldom laboured in vain. That his excellence may be properly estimated, I recommend a comparison of his *Characters of Women* with Boileau's Satire; it will then be seen with how much more perspicacity female nature is investigated, and female excellence selected; and he surely is no mean writer to whom Boileau shall be found inferior. The *Characters of Men,* however, are written with more, if not with deeper thought, and exhibit many passages exquisitely beautiful. The "Gem and the Flower" will not easily be equalled. In the women's part are some defects: the character of Atossa is not so neatly finished as that of Clodio; and some of the female characters may be found perhaps more frequently among men; what is said of Philomede was true of Prior.

In the Epistles to Lord Bathurst and Lord Burlington, Dr. Warburton has endeavoured to find a train of thought which was never in the writer's head, and, to support his hypothesis, has printed that first which was published last. In one, the most valuable passage is perhaps the Elegy on "Good Sense"; and the other, the "End of the Duke of Buckingham."

The *Epistle to Arbuthnot,* now arbitrarily called the *Prologue to the Satires,* is a performance consisting, as it seems, of many fragments wrought into one design, which by this union of scattered beauties contains more striking paragraphs than could probably have been brought together into an occasional work. As there is no stronger motive to exertion than self-defence, no part has more elegance, spirit, or dignity than the poet's vindication of his own character. The meanest passage is the satire upon Sporus.

Of the two poems which derived their names from the year, and which are called the *Epilogue to the Satires,* it was very justly remarked by Savage, that the second was in the whole more strongly conceived, and more equally supported, but that it had no single passages equal to the contention in the first for the dignity of Vice, and the celebration of the triumph of Corruption.

The *Imitations of Horace* seem to have been written as relaxations of his genius. This employment became his favourite by its facility; the plan was ready to his hand, and nothing was required but to accommodate as he could the sentiments of an old author to recent facts or familiar images; but what is easy is seldom excellent; such imitations cannot give pleasure to common readers; the man of learning may be sometimes surprised and delighted by an unexpected parallel; but the comparison requires knowledge of the original, which will likewise often detect strained applications. Between Roman images and English manners there will be an irreconcileable dissimilitude, and the works will be generally uncouth and party-coloured; neither original nor translated, neither ancient nor modern.

[He published likewise a revival, in smoother numbers, of Dr. Donne's *Satires,* which was recommended to him by the Duke of Shrewsbury and the Earl of Oxford. They made no great impression on the public. Pope seems to have known their imbecility, and therefore suppressed them while he was yet contending to rise in reputation, but ventured them when he thought their deficiencies more likely to be imputed to Donne than to himself. . . .

He laid aside his epic poem, perhaps without much loss to mankind; for his hero was Brutus the Trojan, who, according to

a ridiculous fiction, established a colony in Britain. The subject therefore was of the fabulous age; the actors were a race upon whom imagination has been exhausted and attention wearied, and to whom the mind will not easily be recalled when it is invited in blank verse, which Pope had adopted with great imprudence, and I think without due consideration of the nature of our language. . . .]

Pope had, in proportions very nicely adjusted to each other, all the qualities that constitute genius. He had *Invention,* by which new trains of events are formed, and new scenes of imagery displayed, as in *The Rape of the Lock;* and by which extrinsic and adventitious embellishments and illustrations are connected with a known subject, as in the *Essay on Criticism.* He had *Imagination,* which strongly impresses on the writer's mind, and enables him to convey to the reader, the various forms of nature, incidents of life, and energies of passion, as in his *Eloisa, Windsor Forest,* and the *Ethic Epistles.* He had *Judgment,* which selects from life or nature what the present purpose requires, and by separating the essence of things from its concomitants, often makes the representation more powerful than the reality: and he had colours of language always before him, ready to decorate his matter with every grace of elegant expression, as when he accommodates his diction to the wonderful multiplicity of Homer's sentiments and descriptions.

Poetical expression includes sound as well as meaning. "Music," says Dryden, "is inarticulate poetry"; among the excellences of Pope, therefore, must be mentioned the melody of his metre. By perusing the works of Dryden, he discovered the most perfect fabric of English verse, and habituated himself to that only which he found the best; in consequence of which restraint, his poetry has been censured as too uniformly musical, and as glutting the ear with unvaried sweetness. I suspect this objection to be the cant of those who judge by principles rather than perception; and who would even themselves have less pleasure in his works, if he had tried to relieve attention by studied discords, or affected to break his lines and vary his pauses.

But though he was thus careful of his versification, he did not oppress his powers with superfluous rigour. He seems to have thought with Boileau, that the practice of writing might be refined till the difficulty should overbalance the advantage. The construction of his language is not always strictly grammatical; with those rhymes which prescription had conjoined he contented himself, without regard to Swift's remonstrances, though there was no striking consonance; nor was he very careful to vary his terminations, or to refuse admission, at a small distance, to the same rhymes.

To Swift's edict for the exclusion of alexandrines and triplets he paid little regard: he admitted them, but, in the opinion of Fenton, too rarely; he uses them more liberally in his translation than his poems.

He has a few double rhymes; and always, I think, unsuccessfully, except once in *The Rape of the Lock*.

Expletives he very early ejected from his verses; but he now and then admits an epithet rather commodious than important.

Each of the six first lines of the Iliad might lose two syllables with very little diminution of the meaning; and sometimes, after all his art and labour, one verse seems to be made for the sake of another. In his latter productions the diction is sometimes vitiated by French idioms, with which Bolingbroke had perhaps infected him.

I have been told that the couplet by which he declared his own ear to be most gratified was this:

Lo, where Maeotis sleeps, and hardly flows
The freezing Tanais through a waste of snows.

But the reason of this preference I cannot discover.

It is remarked by Watts, that there is scarcely a happy combination of words, or a phrase poetically elegant in the English language, which Pope has not inserted into his version of Homer. How he obtained possession of so many beauties of speech, it were desirable to know. That he gleaned from authors, obscure as well as eminent, what he thought brilliant or useful, and preserved it all in a regular collection, is not unlikely. When, in his last years, Hall's Satires were shown him, he wished that he had seen them sooner.

New sentiments and new images others may produce; but to attempt any further improvement of versification will be dangerous. Art and diligence have now done their best, and what shall be added will be the effort of tedious toil and needless curiosity.

After all this, it is surely superfluous to answer the question that has once been asked, Whether Pope was a poet? otherwise than by asking in return, If Pope be not a poet, where is poetry to be found? To circumscribe poetry by a definition will only show the narrowness of the definer, though a definition which shall exclude Pope will not easily be made. Let us look round upon the present time, and back upon the past; let us inquire to whom the voice of mankind has decreed the wreath of poetry; let their productions be examined, and their claim stated, and the pretensions of Pope will be no more disputed. Had he given the world only his version, the name of poet must have been allowed him: if the writer of the Iliad were to class his successors, he would assign a very high place to his translator, without requiring any other evidence of Genius. . . .

The criticism upon Pope's *Epitaphs*, which was printed in *The Universal Visitor*, is placed here, being too minute and particular to be inserted in the Life. . . .

On MRS. CORBET, *who died of a cancer . . .
in her breast*

Here rests a woman, good without pretence,
Blest with plain reason, and with sober sense;

No conquest she, but o'er herself desir'd;
No arts essay'd, but not to be admir'd.
Passion and pride were to her soul unknown,
Convinc'd that virtue only is our own.
So unaffected, so compos'd a mind,
So firm, yet soft, so strong, yet so refin'd,
Heaven, as its purest gold, by tortures tried;
The saint sustain'd it, but the woman died.

I have always considered this as the most valuable of all Pope's epitaphs: the subject of it is a character not discriminated by any shining or eminent peculiarities; yet that which really makes, though not the splendour, the felicity of life, and that which every wise man will choose for his final and lasting companion in the languor of age, in the quiet of privacy, when he departs weary and disgusted from the ostentatious, the volatile, and the vain. Of such a character, which the dull overlook, and the gay despise, it was fit that the value should be made known and the dignity established. Domestic virtue, as it is exerted without great occasions, or conspicuous consequences, in an even unnoted tenor, required the genius of Pope to display it in such a manner as might attract regard and enforce reverence. Who can forbear to lament that this amiable woman has no name in the verses?

If the particular lines of this inscription be examined, it will appear less faulty than the rest. There is scarce one line taken from commonplaces, unless it be that in which *only virtue* is said to be *our own*. I once heard a lady of great beauty and excellence object to the fourth line, that it contained an unnatural and incredible panegyric. Of this let the ladies judge. . . .

The scantiness of human praises can scarcely be made more apparent than by remarking how often Pope has, in the few epitaphs which he composed, found it necessary to borrow from himself. The fourteen epitaphs which he has written comprise about a hundred and forty lines, in which there are more repetitions than will easily be found in all the rest of his works. . . .

On MR. GAY. *In Westminster Abbey,* 1732
Of manners gentle, of affections mild;
In wit, a man; simplicity, a child:
With native humour tempering virtuous rage,
Formed to delight at once and lash the age:
Above temptation, in a low estate,
And uncorrupted, ev'n among the Great:
A safe companion, and an easy friend,
Unblamed through life, lamented in thy end.
These are thy honours! not that here thy bust
Is mixed with heroes, or with kings thy dust;
But that the Worthy and the Good shall say,
Striking their pensive bosoms—Here lies GAY.

As Gay was the favourite of our author, this epitaph was probably written with an uncommon degree of attention; yet it is not more successfully executed than the rest, for it will not always happen that the success of a poet is proportionate to his labour. The same observation may be extended to all works of imagination, which are often influenced by causes wholly out of the performer's power, by hints of which he perceives not the origin, by sudden elevations of mind which he cannot produce in himself, and which sometimes rise when he expects them least.

The two parts of the first line are only echoes of each other; *gentle manners* and *mild affections,* if they mean anything, must mean the same.

That Gay was a *man in wit* is a very frigid commendation; to have the wit of a man is not much for a poet. The *wit of man,* and the *simplicity of a child,* make a poor and vulgar contrast, and raise no ideas of excellence, either intellectual or moral.

In the next couplet *rage* is less properly introduced after the mention of *mildness* and *gentleness,* which are made the constituents of his character; for a man so *mild* and *gentle* to *temper* his *rage,* was not difficult.

The next line is inharmonious in its sound, and mean in its conception; the opposition is obvious, and the word *lash,* used absolutely and without any modification, is gross and improper.

To be *above temptation* in poverty and *free from corruption among the great*, is indeed such a peculiarity as deserved notice. But to be a *safe companion* is a praise merely negative, arising not from possession of virtue, but the absence of vice, and that one of the most odious.

As little can be added to his character by asserting that he was *lamented in his end*. Every man that dies is, at least by the writer of his epitaph, supposed to be lamented, and therefore this general lamentation does no honour to Gay.

The first eight lines have no grammar; the adjectives are without any substantive, and the epithets without a subject.

The thought in the last line, that Gay is buried in the bosoms of the *worthy* and the *good*, who are distinguished only to lengthen the line, is so dark that few understand it; and so harsh when it is explained, that still fewer approve.

William Cowper

from Table Talk

Then Pope, as harmony itself exact,
In verse well disciplin'd, complete, compact,
Gave virtue and morality a grace,
That, quite eclipsing pleasure's painted face,
Levied a tax of wonder and applause,
Ev'n on the fools that trampled on their laws.
But he (his musical finesse was such,
So nice his ear, so delicate his touch)
Made poetry a mere mechanic art;
And ev'ry warbler has his tune by heart.

(Lines 646–655)

(1782); reprinted from *Poetical Works*, ed. H. S. Milford, London, Oxford University Press, 1926.

William Wordsworth

Remarks on Pope

PERHAPS in no way, by positive example, could more easily be given a notion of what I mean by the phrase *poetic diction* than by referring to a comparison between the metrical paraphrase which we have of passages in the Old and New Testament, and those passages as they exist in our common Translation. See Pope's "Messiah" throughout.

(Appendix to *Lyrical Ballads*, 1802) [1]

I have a very high admiration of the talents both of Dryden and Pope, and ultimately, as from all good writers of whatever kind, their Country will be benefited greatly by their labours. But thus far . . . their writings have done more harm than good. It will require yet half a century completely to carry off the poison of Pope's Homer.

(Letter to Walter Scott, 1808) [2]

The course which we have taken having brought us to the name of this distinguished Writer—Pope—I will in this place give a few observations upon his Epitaphs, —the largest collection we have in our language, from the pen of any Writer of eminence. As the epitaphs of Pope and also those of Chiabrera, which occasioned this dissertation, are in metre, it may be proper here to enquire how far the notion of a perfect epitaph . . . may be modified by the choice of metre for the vehicle, in preference to prose. . . . When I come to the epitaphs of Chiabrera, I shall perhaps give instances in which I think he has not

[1] *Poetical Works*, ed. E. de Selincourt, London, Oxford University Press, 1944, II, 407.

[2] This passage and all subsequent ones are from Markham L. Peacock, Jr., *The Critical Opinions of William Wordsworth*, Baltimore, The Johns Hopkins Press, 1950.

written under the impression of this truth [i.e., that in epitaphs, the occasion forbids "all modes of fiction, except those which the very strength of passion has created"]; where the poetic imagery does not elevate, deepen, or refine the human passion, which it ought always to do or not act at all, but excludes it. In a far greater degree are Pope's epitaphs debased by faults into which he could not I think have fallen if he had written in prose as a plain man and not as a metrical Wit. . . . [In the epitaph on Mrs. Corbet,] the thoughts have their nature changed and moulded by the vicious expression in which they are entangled, to an excess rendering them wholly unfit for the place they occupy.

Here rests a woman, good without pretence,
Blest with plain reason—

from which *sober sense* is not sufficiently distinguishable. This verse and a half, and the one "so unaffected, so composed a mind," are characteristic, and the expression is true to nature; but they are . . . the only parts of the epitaph which have this merit. . . . She is not praised so much as others are blamed, and is degraded by the Author in thus being made a covert or stalking-horse for gratifying a propensity the most abhorrent from her own nature—"Passion and pride were to her soul unknown." . . . If she was "good without pretence," it seems unnecessary to say that she was not proud. Dr. Johnson, making an exception of the verse, "Convinced that virtue only is our own," praises this epitaph for "containing nothing taken from common places." . . . It is not only no fault but a primary requisite in an epitaph that it shall contain thoughts and feelings which are in their substance commonplace, and even trite. It is grounded upon the universal intellectual property of man,—[universal sensations and truths] . . . should be uttered in such connection as shall make it felt that they are not adopted, not spoken by rote, but perceived in their whole compass with the freshness and clearness of an original intuition. . . . The line "Virtue only is our own,"—is objectionable, not from the commonplaceness of the truth, but from the vapid manner in which it is conveyed. . . . "So firm yet soft, so strong yet so refined": These intellectual operations (while they can be conceived of as operations of intellect at all, for in fact one half of the process is mechanical, words doing their own work and one half of the line manufacturing the rest) remind me of the motions of a Posture-master, or of a man balancing a sword upon his finger, which must be kept from falling at all hazards. "The saint sustained it, but the woman died." Let us look steadily at this antithesis: the *saint*, that is her soul strengthened by religion, supported the anguish of her disease with patience and resignation; but the *woman*, that is her body (for if anything else is meant by the word woman, it contradicts the former part of the proposition and the passage is nonsense,) was overcome. Why was not this simply expressed; without playing with the Reader's fancy, to the delusion and dishonour of his understanding, by a trifling epigrammatic point? But alas! ages must pass away before men will have their eyes open to the beauty and majesty of Truth, and will be taught to venerate Poetry no further than as she is a handmaid pure as her mistress—the noblest handmaid in her train! . . .

If my notions are right, the epitaphs of Pope cannot well be too severely condemned; for not only are they almost wholly destitute of those universal feelings and simple movements of mind which we have called for as indispensable, but they are little better than a tissue of false thoughts, languid and vague expressions, unmeaning antithesis, and laborious attempts at discrimination. Pope's mind has been employed chiefly in observation upon the vices and follies of men. Now, vice and folly are in contradiction with the moral principle which can never be extinguished in the mind; and therefore, wanting the contrast, are irregular, capricious, and inconsistent with themselves. . . .

It is reasonable then that Cicero, when holding up Catiline to detestation; and (without going to such an extreme case) that Dryden and Pope, when they are describing characters like Buckingham, Shaftsbury, and the Duchess of Marlborough, should represent qualities and actions at war with each other and with themselves; and that the page should be suitably crowded with antithetical expressions. But all this argues an obtuse moral sensibility and a consequent want of knowledge, if applied where virtue ought to be described in the language of affectionate admiration. In the mind of the truly great and good everything that is of importance is at peace with itself; all is stillness, sweetness and stable grandeur. Accordingly the contemplation of virtue is attended with repose.

("Essays [2 and 3] on Epitaphs," 1810)

The arts by which Pope contrived to procure himself a more general and a higher reputation than perhaps any English Poet ever attained during his lifetime, are known to the judicious. And as well known is it to them, that the undue exertion of those arts is the cause why Pope has for some time held a rank in literature, to which, if he had not been seduced by an over-love of immediate popularity, and had confided more in his native genius, he never could have descended. He bewitched the nation by his melody, and dazzled it by his polished style, and was himself blinded by his own success. Having wandered from humanity in his Eclogues with boyish inexperience, the praise, which these compositions obtained, tempted him into a belief that Nature was not to be trusted, at least in pastoral Poetry. To prove this by example, he put his friend Gay upon writing those Eclogues which their author intended to be burlesque. The instigator of the work, and his admirers, could perceive in them nothing but what was ridiculous. Nevertheless, though these Poems contain some detestable passages, the effect, as Dr. Johnson well observes, "of reality and truth became conspicuous even when the intention was to show them grovelling and degraded." The Pastorals, ludicrous to such as prided themselves upon their refinement, in spite of those disgusting passages, "became popular, and were read with delight, as just representations of rural manners and occupations." . . .

Now, it is remarkable that, excepting the nocturnal *Reverie* of Lady Winchelsea, and a passage or two in the *Windsor Forest* of Pope, the poetry of the period intervening between the publication of the *Paradise Lost* and the *Seasons* does not contain a single new image of external nature; and scarcely presents a familiar one from which it can be inferred that the eye of the Poet had been steadily fixed upon his object, much less that his feelings had urged him to work upon it in the spirit of genuine imagination. To what a low state knowledge of the most obvious and important phenomena had sunk, is evident from the style in which Dryden has executed a description of Night in one of his Tragedies [*The Indian Emperor*, III, ii, 1–6], and Pope his translation of the celebrated moonlight scene in the *Iliad* [conclusion of Book VIII]. A blind man, in the habit of attending accurately to descriptions casually dropped from the lips of those around him, might easily depict these appearances with more truth. Dryden's lines are vague, bombastic, and senseless; those of Pope, though he had Homer to guide him, are throughout false and contradictory. The verses of Dryden, once

highly celebrated, are forgotten; those of Pope still retain their hold upon public estimation,—nay, there is not a passage of descriptive poetry, which at this day finds so many and such ardent admirers. Strange to think of an enthusiast, as may have been the case with thousands, reciting those verses under the cope of a moonlight sky, without having his raptures in the least disturbed by a suspicion of their absurdity!—If these two distinguished writers could habitually think that the visible universe was of so little consequence to a poet, that it was scarcely necessary for him to cast his eyes upon it, we may be assured that those passages of the elder poets which faithfully and poetically describe the phenomena of nature, were not at that time holden in much estimation, and that there was little accurate attention paid to those appearances.

("Essay Supplementary to the Preface" to *Lyrical Ballads*, 1815)

Pope, in that production of his Boyhood, the ode to Solitude, and in his Essay on Criticism, has furnished proofs that at one period of his life he felt the charm of a sober and subdued style, which he afterwards abandoned for one that is to my taste at least too pointed and ambitious, and for a versification too timidly balanced.

(Letter to Dyce, 1830)

I have ten times more knowledge of Pope's writings, and of Dryden's also, than ever this writer [Hazlitt] had. To this day I believe I could repeat, with a little previous rummaging of my memory, several thousand lines of Pope. But if the beautiful, the pathetic, and the sublime be what a poet should chiefly aim at, how absurd it is to place these men amongst the first poets of their country! Admirable are they in treading their way, but that way lies almost at the foot of Parnassus.

(Opinion of 1836 or later, recorded in *Letters of the Wordsworth Family*)

Samuel Taylor Coleridge

Remarks on Pope

[OF Chapman's translation of Homer's *Odyssey*:] Excepting his quaint epithets which he affects to render literally from the Greek, . . . it has no look, no air, of a translation. It is as truly an original poem as the Faery Queene;—it will give you small idea of Homer, though a far truer one than Pope's epigrams, or Cowper's cumbersome most anti-Homeric Miltonism. For Chapman writes and feels as a poet,—as Homer might have written had he lived in England in the reign of Queen Elizabeth.

("Notes on Chapman's Homer,"
in letter to Wordsworth, 1807) [1]

Among those with whom I conversed [at sixteen], there were, of course, very many who had formed their taste, and their notions of poetry, from the writings of Mr. Pope and his followers: or to speak more generally, in that school of French poetry, condensed and invigorated by English understanding, which had predominated from the last century. I was not blind to the merits of this school, yet as from inexperience of the world, and consequent want of sympathy with the general subjects of these poems, they gave me little pleasure, I doubtless undervalued the *kind,* and with the presumption of youth withheld from its masters the legitimate name of poets. I saw that the excellence of this kind consisted in just and acute observations on men and manners in an artificial state of society, as its matter and substance: and in the logic of wit, conveyed in smooth and strong epigrammatic couplets, as its *form.* Even when the subject

[1] *Complete Works,* ed. W. G. T. Shedd, New York, Harper & Brothers, 1884, IV, 373.

was addressed to the fancy, or the intellect, as in the Rape of the Lock, or the Essay on Man; nay, when it was a consecutive narration, as in that astonishing product of matchless talent and ingenuity, Pope's Translation of the Iliad; still a *point* was looked for at the end of each second line, and the whole was as it were a sorites, or, if I may exchange a logical for a grammatical metaphor, a *conjunction disjunctive,* of epigrams. Meantime the matter and diction seemed to me characterized not so much by poetic thoughts, as by thoughts *translated* into the language of poetry. . . .

In the course of one of my Lectures, I had occasion to point out the almost faultless position and choice of words, in Mr. Pope's *original* compositions, particularly in his Satires and moral Essays, for the purpose of comparing them with his translation of Homer, which I do not stand alone in regarding as the main source of our pseudo-poetic diction. And this, by the bye, is an additional confirmation of a remark made, I believe, by Sir Joshua Reynolds, that next to the man who forms and elevates the taste of the public, he that corrupts it, is commonly the greatest genius. Among other passages, I analyzed sentence by sentence, and almost word by word, the popular lines,

"As when the moon, resplendent lamp of light [*sic*], &c."

[*Iliad*, VIII, 555]

. . . The impression on the audience in general was sudden and evident: and a number of enlightened and highly educated persons . . . expressed their wonder, that truth so obvious should not have struck them *before;* but at the same time acknowledged . . . that they might in all probability have read the same passage again twenty times with undiminished admiration, and without once reflecting, that "ἄστρα φαεινὴν ἀμφὶ σελήνην φαίνετ' ἀριπρεπέα" (i.e. the stars around, or near the full moon, shine pre-eminently bright) conveys a just and happy image of a moonlight sky: while it is difficult to determine whether, in the lines,

"Around *her throne* the vivid planets *roll,*
And stars *unnumber'd gild* the *glowing pole,*"

the sense or the diction be the more absurd. . . .

[On Pope's translation of the passage where the sight of Achilles' shield to Priam is compared with the Dog Star:]

"Terrific Glory! for his burning breath
Taints the *red* air with fevers, plagues, and death!"
[*Iliad*, XXII, 41–42]

Now here (not to mention the tremendous bombast) the *Dog Star*, so called, is turned into a *real Dog*, a very odd Dog, a Fire, Fever, Plague, and death-breathing, *red*-air-tainting Dog: and the whole *visual* likeness is lost, while the likeness in the *effects* is rendered absurd by the exaggeration. . . .

The language [of English poetry] from Pope's "Translation of Homer" to Darwin's "Temple of Nature," may, notwithstanding some illustrious exceptions, be too faithfully characterized, as claiming to be poetical for no better reason, than that it would be intolerable in conversation or in prose.

(*Biographia Literaria*, 1817, chs. I, II, XVI) [2]

It is the existence of an individual idiom in each, that makes the principal [prose] writers before the Restoration the great

patterns or integers of English style. In them the precise intended meaning of a word can never be mistaken; whereas in the latter writers, as especially in Pope, the use of words is for the most part purely arbitrary, so that the context will rarely show the true specific sense, but only that something of the sort is designed.

(Lecture "On Style," 1818) [3]

You will find this a good gauge or criterion of genius—whether it progresses and evolves, or only spins upon itself. Take Dryden's Achitophel and Zimri—Shaftesbury and Buckingham; every line adds to or modifies the character, which is, as it were, a-building up to the very last verse; whereas, in Pope's Timon, &c., the first two or three couplets contain all the pith of the character, and the twenty or thirty lines that follow are so much evidence or proof of overt acts of jealousy, or pride, or whatever it may be that is satirized.

("Table Talk," 1832) [4]

[Quotes Selden: "The old poets had no other reason but this, their verse was sung to music: otherwise it had been a senseless thing to have fettered up themselves."] No man can know all things: even Selden here talks ignorantly. Verse is in itself a music, and the natural symbol of that union of passion with thought and pleasure, which constitutes the essence of all poetry, as contra-distinguished from science, and distinguished from history civil or natural. To Pope's Essay on Man,—in short, to whatever is mere metrical good sense and wit the remark applies.

("Notes on Selden's Table Talk") [5]

[3] *Complete Works*, IV, 340–341.
[4] *The Table Talk and Omniana of Samuel Taylor Coleridge*, London, Oxford University Press, 1917, p. 194.
[5] *Complete Works*, IV, 379. (Ed. note in this edition: "These remarks on Selden were communicated by Mr. Cary.")

[2] Ed. J. Shawcross, London, Oxford University Press, 1907, I, 11, 26–27, 33; II, 21.

William Blake

Imitation of Pope: A Compliment to the Ladies

Wondrous the Gods, more wondrous are the Men,
More Wondrous Wondrous still the Cock & Hen,
More Wondrous still the Table, Stool & Chair;
But Ah! More wondrous still the Charming Fair.

(c. 1808) ; reprinted from *Complete Writings*, ed. Geoffrey Keynes, London, Nonesuch Press, 1957, p. 545. (J. E. Grant brought this poem to my attention.—Ed.)

George Gordon, Lord Byron

from English Bards and Scotch Reviewers

Bowles! in thy memory let this precept dwell,
Stick to thy sonnets, man!—at least they sell.
But if some new-born whim, or larger bribe,
Prompt thy crude brain, and claim thee for a scribe;
If chance some bard, though once by dunces fear'd,
Now, prone in dust, can only be revered;
If Pope, whose fame and genius from the first
Have foil'd the best of critics, needs the worst,
Do thou essay: each fault, each failing scan;
The first of poets was, alas! but man.
Rake from each ancient dunghill ev'ry pearl,
Consult Lord Fanny, and confide in Curll;
Let all the scandals of a former age
Perch on thy pen, and flutter o'er thy page;
Affect a candour which thou canst not feel,
Clothe envy in the garb of honest zeal;
Write, as if St. John's soul could still inspire,
And do from hate what Mallet did for hire.
Oh! hadst thou lived in that congenial time,
To rave with Dennis, and with Ralph to rhyme;
Throng'd with the rest around his living head,
Not raised thy hoof against the lion dead;
A meet reward had crown'd thy glorious gains,
And link'd thee to the Dunciad for thy pains.
                    (Lines 361–384)

(2nd ed., 1809) ; reprinted from *Complete Poetical Works*, ed. Paul Elmer More, Boston, Houghton Mifflin Company (Cambridge Edition), 1905, pp. 246–247.

Some Observations upon an Article in *Blackwood's Magazine*

I WISH to say a few words on the present state of English poetry. That this is the age of the decline of English poetry will be doubted by few who have calmly considered the subject. That there are men of genius among the present poets makes little against the fact, because it has been well said, that "next to him who forms the taste of his country, the greatest genius is he who corrupts it." No one has ever denied genius to Marino, who corrupted not merely the taste of Italy, but that of all Europe for nearly a century. The great cause of the present deplorable state of English poetry is to be attributed to that absurd and systematic depreciation of Pope, in which, for the last few years, there has been a kind of epidemical concurrence. Men of the most opposite opinions have united upon this topic. Warton and Churchill began it, having borrowed the hint probably from the heroes of the *Dunciad,* and their own internal conviction that their proper reputation can be as nothing till the most perfect and harmonious of poets—he who, having no fault, has had REASON made his reproach—was reduced to what they conceived to be his level. . . .

Southey, Wordsworth, and Coleridge, had all of them a very natural antipathy to Pope; and I respect them for it, as the only original feeling or principle which they have contrived to preserve. But they have been joined in it by those who have joined them in nothing else: by the Edinburgh Reviewers, by the whole heterogeneous mass of living English poets, excepting Crabbe, Rogers, Gifford, and Campbell, who, both by precept and practice, have proved their adherence; and by me, who have shamefully deviated in practice, but have ever loved and honoured Pope's poetry with my whole soul, and hope to do so till my dying day. I would rather see all I have ever written lining the same trunk in which I actually read the eleventh book of a modern epic poem at Malta, in 1811, (I opened it to take out a change after the paroxysm of a tertian, in the absence of my servant, and found it lined with the name of the maker, Eyre, Cockspur Street, and with the epic poetry alluded to,) than sacrifice what I firmly believe in as the Christianity of English poetry, the poetry of Pope.

But the Edinburgh Reviewers, and the Lakers, and Hunt and his school, and every body else with their school, and even Moore without a school, and dilettanti lecturers at institutions, and elderly gentlemen who translate and imitate, and young ladies who listen and repeat, baronets who draw indifferent frontispieces for bad poets, and noblemen who let them dine with them in the country, the small body of wits and the great body of the blues, have latterly united in a depreciation, of which their fathers would have been as much ashamed as their children will be. . . .

There are, I trust, younger spirits rising up in England, who, escaping the contagion which has swept away poetry from our literature, will recall it to their country, such as it once was and may still be.

In the mean time, the best sign of amendment will be repentance, and new and frequent editions of Pope and Dryden.

There will be found as comfortable metaphysics, and ten times more poetry in the *Essay on Man,* than in the *Excursion.* If you search for passion, where is it to be

(1820); reprinted from *Works: Letters and Journals,* ed. Rowland E. Prothero, London, John Murray, IV (1900), 484–493.

found stronger than in the epistle to Eloisa from Abelard, or in *Palamon and Arcite?* Do you wish for invention, imagination, sublimity, character? seek them in the *Rape of the Lock*, the *Fables* of Dryden, the *Ode of Saint Cecilia's Day*, and *Absalom and Achitophel:* you will discover in these two poets only, *all* for which you must ransack innumerable metres, and God only knows how many *writers* of the day, without finding a tittle of the same qualities,—with the addition, too, of wit, of which the latter have none. . . . I will say nothing of the harmony of Pope and Dryden in comparison, for there is not a living poet (except Rogers, Gifford, Campbell, and Crabbe,) who can write an heroic couplet. The fact is, that the exquisite beauty of their versification has withdrawn the public attention from their other excellences, as the vulgar eye will rest more upon the splendour of the uniform than the quality of the troops. It is this very harmony, particularly in Pope, which has raised the vulgar and atrocious cant against him:—because his versification is perfect, it is assumed that it is his only perfection; because his truths are so clear, it is asserted that he has no invention; and because he is always intelligible, it is taken for granted that he has no genius. We are sneeringly told that he is the "Poet of Reason," as if this was a reason for his being no poet. Taking passage for passage, I will undertake to cite more lines teeming with *imagination* from Pope than from any *two* living poets, be they who they may. To take an instance at random from a species of composition not very favourable to imagination—Satire: set down the character of Sporus, with all the wonderful play of fancy which is scattered over it, and place by its side an equal number of verses, from any two existing poets, of the same power and the same variety—where will you find them? . . .

To the heaven-born genii and inspired young scriveners of the day much of this will appear paradox: it will appear so even to the higher order of our critics; but it was a truism twenty years ago, and it will be a reacknowledged truth in ten more. In the mean time, I will conclude with . . . [a quotation] from the volume of a young person learning to write poetry, and beginning by teaching the art. Hear him—

> "But ye were dead
> To things ye knew not of—were closely wed
> To musty laws lined out with wretched rule
> And compass vile; so that ye taught a school
> Of *dolts* to *smooth, inlay,* and *chip,* and *fit,*
> Till, like the certain wands of Jacob's wit,
> *Their verses tallied. Easy was the task:*
> A thousand handicraftsmen wore the mask
> Of poesy. Ill-fated, impious race,
> That blasphemed the bright lyrist to his face,
> And did not know it; no, they went about
> Holding a poor *decrepit* standard out
> Mark'd with most flimsy mottos, and in large
> The name of *one* Boileau!"

A little before, the manner of Pope is termed,

> "A *scism,*
> Nurtured by *foppery* and barbarism,
> Made great Apollo blush for this his land." [1]

I thought *"foppery,"* was a consequence of *refinement,* but *n'importe.*

The above will suffice to show the notions entertained by the new performers on the English lyre of him who made it most tuneable, and the great improvements of their own "variazioni."

The writer of this is a tadpole of the Lakes, a young disciple of the six or seven new schools, in which he has learnt to write such lines and such sentiments as the above. He says "easy was the task" of imitating Pope, or it may be of equalling him, I presume. I recommend him to try before he is so positive on the subject, and then compare what he will have *then* written

[1] As a balance to these lines, and to the sense and sentiment of the new school, I will put down a passage or two from Pope's *earliest* poems, taken at random . . . [quotes *Windsor Forest,* lines 419–422, 115–118, 69–72; *Essay on Criticism,* lines 189–200, 247–252; *Temple of Fame,* lines 85–88, 53–60].

and what he has *now* written with the humblest and earliest compositions of Pope, produced in years still more youthful than those of Mr. Keats when he invented his new "Essay on Criticism," entitled *Sleep*

and Poetry (an ominous title,) from whence the above canons are taken. Pope's was written at nineteen, and published at twenty-two.

On One of Bowles's Strictures on Pope

To the question, "Whether the description of a game of cards be as poetical, supposing the execution of the artists equal, as a description of a walk in a forest?" it may be answered, that the *materials* are certainly not equal; but that "the *artist*," who has rendered the "game of cards poetical," is *by far the greater* of the two.

From *Letter to* **** ****** [John Murray] (1821), in *Letters and Journals*, V (1901), 552–553. Byron is retorting to the following statement by W. L. Bowles: "The descriptive poet, who paints from an intimate knowledge of external nature, is more poetical, supposing the fidelity and execution equal, *not* than the painter of human passions, but the painter of external circumstances in artificial life; as Cowper paints a morning walk, and Pope a game of cards!" (*The Invariable Principles of Poetry*, 1819; quoted ibid., p. 532).

William Hazlitt

On Dryden and Pope

DRYDEN and Pope are the great masters of the artificial style of poetry in our language, as the poets of whom I have already treated, Chaucer, Spenser, Shakspeare, and Milton, were of the natural; and though this artificial style is generally and very justly acknowledged to be inferior to the other, yet those who stand at the head of that class ought, perhaps, to rank higher than those who occupy an inferior place in a superior class. They have a clear and independent claim upon our gratitude, as having produced a kind and degree of excellence which existed equally nowhere else. What has been done well by some later writers of the highest style of poetry, is included in, and obscured by, a greater degree of power and genius in those before them: what has been done best by poets of an entirely distinct turn of mind, stands by itself, and tells for its whole amount. Young, for instance, Gray, or Akenside, only follow in the train of Milton and Shakspeare: Pope and Dryden walk by their side, though of an unequal stature, and are entitled to a first place in the lists of fame. This seems to be not only the reason of the thing, but the common sense of mankind, who, without any regular process of reflection, judge of the merit of a work not more by its inherent and absolute worth than by its originality and capacity of gratifying a different faculty of the mind, or a different class of readers; for it should be recollected that there may be readers (as well as poets) not of the highest class, though very good sort of people, and not altogether to be despised.

The question, whether Pope was a poet, has hardly yet been settled, and is hardly worth settling; for, if he was not a great poet, he must have been a great prose writer, that is, he was a great writer of some sort. He was a man of exquisite faculties, and of the most refined taste; and as he chose verse (the most obvious distinction of poetry) as the vehicle to express his ideas, he has generally passed for a poet, and a good one. If, indeed, by a great poet, we mean one who gives the utmost grandeur to our conceptions of nature, or the utmost force to the passions of the heart, Pope was not in this sense a great poet; for the bent, the characteristic power of his mind, lay the clean contrary way; namely, in representing things as they appear to the indifferent observer, stripped of prejudice and passion, as in his Critical Essays; or in representing them in the most contemptible and insignificant point of view, as in his Satires; or in clothing the little with mock-dignity, as in his poems of Fancy; or in adorning the trivial incidents and familiar relations of life with the utmost elegance of expression, and all the flattering illusions of friendship or self-love, as in his Epistles. He was not then distinguished as a poet of lofty enthusiasm, of strong imagination, with a passionate sense of the beauties of nature, or a deep insight into the workings of the heart; but he was a wit, and a critic, a man of sense, of observation, and the world, with a keen relish for the elegances of art, or of nature when embellished by art, a quick tact for propriety of thought and manners as estab-

From *Lectures on the English Poets* (1818–19) ; reprinted from *Miscellaneous Works*, 3 vols., Philadelphia, J. B. Lippincott, n. d., III, 82–95. (Bracketed passages are from other works in the same volume.)

lished by the forms and customs of society, refined sympathy with the sentiments and habitudes of human life, as he felt them within the little circle of his family and friends. He was, in a word, the poet, not of nature, but of art; and the distinction between the two, as well as I can make it out, is this:—The poet of nature is one who from the elements of beauty, of power, and of passion in his own breast, sympathises with whatever is beautiful, and grand, and impassioned in nature, in its simple majesty, in its immediate appeal to the senses, to the thoughts and hearts of all men; so that the poet of nature, by the truth, and depth, and harmony of his mind, may be said to hold communion with the very soul of nature; to be identified with, and to foreknow, and to record, the feelings of all men, at all times and places, as they are liable to the same impressions; and to exert the same power over the minds of his readers that nature does. He sees things in their eternal beauty, for he sees them as they are; he feels them in their universal interest, for he feels them as they affect the first principles of his and our common nature. Such was Homer, such was Shakspeare, whose works will last as long as nature, because they are a copy of the indestructible forms and everlasting impulses of nature, welling out from the bosom as from a perennial spring, or stamped upon the senses by the hand of their Maker. The power of the imagination in them is the representative power of all nature. It has its centre in the human soul, and makes the circuit of the universe.

Pope was not assuredly a poet of this class, or in the first rank of it. He saw nature only dressed by art; he judged of beauty by fashion; he sought for truth in the opinions of the world; he judged of the feelings of others by his own. The capacious soul of Shakspeare had an intuitive and mighty sympathy with whatever could enter into the heart of man in all possible circumstances: Pope had an exact knowledge of all that he himself loved or hated, wished or wanted. Milton has winged his daring flight from heaven to earth, through Chaos and old Night. Pope's Muse never wandered with safety, but from his library to his grotto, or from his grotto into his library back again. His mind dwelt with greater pleasure on his own garden than on the garden of Eden; he could describe the faultless whole-length mirror that reflected his own person better than the smooth surface of the lake that reflects the face of heaven—a piece of cut glass or a pair of paste buckles with more brilliance and effect than a thousand dew-drops glittering in the sun. He would be more delighted with a patent lamp than with "the pale reflex of Cynthia's brow," that fills the skies with its soft silent lustre, that trembles through the cottage window, and cheers the watchful mariner on the lonely wave. In short, he was the poet of personality and of polished life. That which was nearest to him was the greatest; the fashion of the day bore sway in his mind over the immutable laws of nature. He preferred the artificial to the natural in external objects, because he had a stronger fellow-feeling with the self-love of the maker or proprietor of a gewgaw than admiration of that which was interesting to all mankind. He preferred the artificial to the natural in passion, because the involuntary and uncalculating impulses of the one hurried him away with a force and vehemence with which he could not grapple; while he could trifle with the conventional and superficial modifications of mere sentiment at will, laugh at or admire, put them on or off like a masquerade-dress, make much or little of them, indulge them for a longer or a shorter time, as he pleased; and because, while they amused his fancy and exercised his ingenuity, they never once disturbed his vanity, his levity, or indifference. His mind was the antithesis of strength and grandeur; its power was the power of indifference. He had none of the enthusiasm of poetry; he was in poetry what the sceptic is in religion.

It cannot be denied that his chief excellence lay more in diminishing than in aggrandizing objects; in checking, not in encouraging, our enthusiasm; in sneering at the extravagances of fancy or passion, instead of giving a loose to them; in describing a row of pins and needles rather than the embattled spears of Greeks and Trojans; in penning a lampoon or a compliment, and in praising Martha Blount.

Shakspeare says,

> "———In Fortune's ray and brightness
> The herd hath more annoyance by the brize
> Than by the tyger: but when the splitting wind
> Makes flexible the knees of knotted oaks,
> And flies fled under shade, why then
> The thing of courage,
> As roused with rage, with rage doth sympathise
> And, with an accent tuned in the self-same key,
> Replies to chiding Fortune."

There is none of this rough work in Pope. His Muse was on a peace-establishment, and grew somewhat effeminate by long ease and indulgence. He lived in the smiles of fortune, and basked in the favour of the great. In his smooth and polished verse we meet with no prodigies of nature, but with miracles of wit; the thunders of his pen are whispered flatteries; its forked lightnings pointed sarcasms; for "the gnarled oak," he gives us "the soft myrtle:" for rocks, and seas, and mountains, artificial grass-plats, gravel-walks, and tinkling rills; for earthquakes and tempests, the breaking of a flower-pot, or the fall of a china jar; for the tug and war of the elements, or the deadly strife of the passions, we have

> "Calm contemplation and poetic ease."

Yet within this retired and narrow circle how much, and that how exquisite, was contained! What discrimination, what wit, what delicacy, what fancy, what lurking spleen, what elegance of thought, what pampered refinement of sentiment! It is like looking at the world through a microscope, where every thing assumes a new character and a new consequence, where things are seen in their minutest circumstances and slightest shades of difference; where the little becomes gigantic, the deformed beautiful, and the beautiful deformed. The wrong end of the magnifier is, to be sure, held to every thing, but still the exhibition is highly curious, and we know not whether to be most pleased or surprised. Such, at least, is the best account I am able to give of this extraordinary man, without doing injustice to him or others. It is time to refer to particular instances in his works.—The Rape of the Lock is the best or more ingenious of these. It is the most exquisite specimen of *fillagree* work ever invented. It is admirable in proportion as it is made of nothing.

> "More subtle web Arachne cannot spin,
> Nor the fine nets, which oft we woven see
> Of scorched dew, do not in th' air more lightly flee."

It is made of gauze and silver spangles. The most glittering appearance is given to every thing, to paste, pomatum, billet-doux, and patches. Airs, languid airs, breathe around; the atmosphere is perfumed with affectation. A toilette is described with the solemnity of an altar raised to the goddess of vanity and the history of a silver bodkin is given with all the pomp of heraldry. No pains are spared, no profusion of ornament, no splendour of poetic diction, to set off the meanest things. The balance between the concealed irony and the assumed gravity is as nicely trimmed as the balance of power in Europe. The little is made great, and the great little. You hardly know whether to laugh or weep. It is the triumph of insignificance, the apotheosis of foppery and folly. It is the perfection of the mock-heroic! . . . The Rape of the Lock is a double-refined essence of wit and fancy, as the Essay on Criticism is of wit and sense. The quantity of thought and observation in this work, for so young a man as Pope was when he wrote it, is wonderful: unless we adopt the supposition that most men of genius spend the rest of their lives in teaching others

hey themselves have learned under
r. The conciseness and felicity of the
expression are equally remarkable. Thus,
on reasoning on the variety of men's opinion, he says—

> " 'Tis with our judgments, as our watches; none
> Go just alike, yet each believes his own."

Nothing can be more original and happy
than the general remarks and illustrations
in the Essay: the critical rules laid down
are too much those of a school, and of a
confined one. There is one passage in the
Essay on Criticism in which the author
speaks with that eloquent enthusiasm of
the fame of ancient writers, which those
will always feel who have themselves any
hope or chance of immortality. . . .

There is a cant in the present day about
genius, as every thing in poetry: there was
a cant in the time of Pope about sense, as
performing all sorts of wonders. It was a
kind of watchword, the shibboleth of a
critical party of the day. As a proof of the
exclusive attention which it occupied in
their minds, it is remarkable that in the
Essay on Criticism (not a very long poem)
there are no less than half a score successive couplets rhyming to the word
sense. . . .

I have mentioned this the more for the
sake of those critics who are bigotted idol-
isers of our author, chiefly on the score of
his correctness. These persons seem to be
of opinion that "there is but one perfect
writer, even Pope." This is, however, a
mistake: his excellence is by no means
faultlessness. If he had no great faults, he
is full of little errors. His grammatical construction is often lame and imperfect. In
the Abelard and Eloise, he says—

> "There died the best of passions, Love and
> Fame."

This is not a legitimate ellipsis. Fame is
not a passion, though love is: but his ear
was evidently confused by the meeting of
the sounds "love and fame," as if they of
themselves immediately implied, "love,

and love of fame." Pope's rhymes are con-
stantly defective, being rhymes to the eye
instead of the ear; and this to a greater
degree, not only than in later, but than in
preceding, writers. The praise of his versification must be confined to its uniform
smoothness and harmony. In the translation of the Iliad, which has been considered as his masterpiece in style and execution, he continually changes the tenses in
the same sentence for the purpose of the
rhyme, which shows either a want of technical resources, or great inattention to
punctilious exactness. But to have done
with this.

The epistle of Eloise to Abelard is the
only exception, I can think of, to the general spirit of the foregoing remarks; and I
should be disingenuous not to acknowledge that it is an exception. The founda-
tion is in the letters themselves of Abelard
and Eloise, which are quite as impressive,
but still in a different way. It is fine as a
poem: it is finer as a piece of high-wrought
eloquence. No woman could be supposed
to write a better love-letter in verse. Besides the richness of the historical materials, the high *gusto* of the original sentiments which Pope had to work upon, there
were perhaps circumstances in his own
situation which made him enter into the
subject with even more than a poet's feeling. The tears shed are drops gushing from
the heart: the words are burning sighs
breathed from the soul of love. Perhaps
the poem to which it bears the greatest
similarity in our language is Dryden's
Tancred and Sigismunda, taken from Boccaccio. Pope's Eloise will bear this comparison; and after such a test, with Boccaccio for the original author, and Dryden for
the translator, it need shrink from no
other. There is something exceedingly tender and beautiful in the sound of the concluding lines:

> "If ever chance two wandering lovers brings
> To Paraclete's white walls and silver springs,"
> &c.

[(Bowles) agrees with Lord Byron that the Epistle to Abelard is the height of the pathetic. . . . That it is in a great degree pathetic, I should be among the last to dispute; but its character is more properly rhetorical and voluptuous. That its interest is of the highest or deepest order is what I should wonder to hear any one affirm who is intimate with Shakspeare, Chaucer, Boccaccio, our own early dramatists, or the Greek tragedians. There is more true, unfeigned, unspeakable, heartfelt distress in one line of Chaucer's tale just mentioned (*The Clerk's Tale,* line 880),

Let me not like a worm go by the way,

than in all Pope's writings put together; and I say it without any disrespect to him, too.] [1]

The Essay on Man is not Pope's best work. It is a theory which Bolingbroke is supposed to have given him, and which he expanded into verse. But "he spins the thread of his verbosity finer than the staple of his argument." All that he says, "the very words, and to the self-same tune," would prove just as well that whatever is is *wrong,* as that whatever is is *right.* The Dunciad has splendid passages, but in general it is dull, heavy, and mechanical. The sarcasm already quoted on Settle, the Lord Mayor's poet (for at that time there was a city, as well as a court, poet,)

"Now night descending, the proud scene is o'er, But lives in Settle's numbers one day more,"—

is the finest inversion of immortality conceivable. [Wit or ludicrous invention produces its effect oftenest by comparison, but not always. . . . The finest piece of wit I know of, is in the lines of Pope on the Lord Mayor's show. . . . It fixes the *maximum* of littleness and insignificance; but it is not by likeness to anything else that it does this, but by literally taking the lowest possible duration of ephemeral reputation, marking it (as with a slider) on the scale

of endless renown, and giving a rival credit for it as his loftiest praise. In a word, the shrewd separation or disentangling of ideas that seem the same, or where the secret contradiction is not sufficiently suspected, and is of a ludicrous and whimsical nature, is wit just as much as the bringing together those that appear at first sight totally different.] [2] It is even better than his serious apostrophe to the great heirs of glory, the triumphant bards of antiquity!

The finest burst of severe moral invective in all Pope is the prophetical conclusion of the epilogue to the Satires.

His Satires are not in general so good as his Epistles. His enmity is effeminate and petulant from a sense of weakness, as his friendship was tender from a sense of gratitude. I do not like, for instance, his character of Chartres, or his characters of women. His delicacy often borders upon sickliness; his fastidiousness makes others fastidious. But his compliments are divine; they are equal in value to a house or an estate. Take the following. In addressing Lord Mansfield, he speaks of the grave as a scene,

"Where Murray, long enough his country's pride,
Shall be no more than Tully, or than Hyde."

To Bolingbroke he says—

"Why rail they then if but one wreath of mine,
Oh all-accomplished St. John, deck thy shrine?"

Again, he has bequeathed this praise to Lord Cornbury—

"Despise low thoughts, low gains:
Disdain whatever Cornbury disdains;
Be virtuous and be happy for your pains."

One would think (though there is no knowing) that a descendant of this nobleman, if there be such a person living, could hardly be guilty of a mean or paltry action.

The finest piece of personal satire in

---

[1] From "Pope, Lord Byron, and Mr. Bowles," *London Magazine,* June, 1821; ibid., p. 254.

[2] From "On Wit and Humour," *Lectures on the English Comic Writers* (1818) ; ibid., pp. 16–17.

Pope (perhaps in the world) is his character of Addison; and this, it may be observed, is of a mixed kind, made up of his respect for the man, and a cutting sense of his failings. The other finest one is that of Buckingham, and the best part of that is the pleasurable.

> "———Alas! how changed from him,
> That life of pleasure and that soul of whim,
> Gallant and gay, in Cliveden's proud alcove,
> The bower of wanton Shrewsbury and love!"

Among his happiest and most inimitable effusions are the Epistles to Arbuthnot, and to Jervas the painter; amiable patterns of the delightful unconcerned life, blending ease with dignity which poets and painters then led. . . .

And shall we cut ourselves off from beauties like these with a theory? Shall we shut up our books, and seal up our senses, to please the dull spite and inordinate vanity of those "who have eyes, but they see not—ears, but they hear not—and understandings, but they understand not,"—and go about asking our blind guides whether Pope was a poet or not? It will never do. Such persons, when you point out to them a fine passage in Pope, turn it off to something of the same sort in some other writer. Thus they say that the line "I lisp'd in numbers, for the numbers came," is pretty, but taken from that of Ovid—*Et quum conabar scribere, versus erat*. They are safe in this mode of criticism: there is no danger of any one's tracing their writings to the classics.

Pope's letters and prose writings neither take away from, nor add to, his poetical reputation. There is, occasionally, a littleness of manner, and an unnecessary degree of caution. He appears anxious to say a good thing in every word, as well as every sentence. They, however, give a very favourable idea of his moral character in all respects; and his letters to Atterbury, in his disgrace and exile, do equal honour to both. If I had to choose, there are one or two persons, and but one or two, that I should like to have been, better than Pope!

Dryden was a better prose-writer, and a bolder and more varied versifier, than Pope. He was a more vigorous thinker, a more correct and logical declaimer, and had more of what may be called strength of mind than Pope; but he had not the same refinement and delicacy of feeling. Dryden's eloquence and spirit were possessed in a higher degree by others, and in nearly the same degree by Pope himself; but that by which Pope was distinguished was an essence which he alone possessed, and of incomparable value on that sole account. Dryden's Epistles are excellent, but inferior to Pope's, though they appear (particularly the admirable one to Congreve) to have been the model on which the latter formed his. His Satires are better than Pope's. His Absalom and Achitophel is superior, both in force of invective and discrimination of character, to anything of Pope's in the same way. The character of Achitophel is very fine; and breathes, if not a sincere love for virtue, a strong spirit of indignation against vice.

Mac Flecknoe is the origin of the idea of the Dunciad; but it is less elaborately constructed, less feeble, and less heavy. The difference between Pope's satirical portraits and Dryden's appears to be this, in a good measure, that Dryden seems to grapple with his antagonists, and to describe real persons; Pope seems to refine upon them in his own mind, and to make them out just what he pleases, till they are not real characters, but the mere driveling effusions of his spleen and malice. Pope describes the thing, and then goes on describing his own description till he loses himself in verbal repetitions. Dryden recurs to the object often, takes fresh sittings of nature, and gives us new strokes of character as well as of his pencil.

William Makepeace Thackeray

The Conclusion of the *Dunciad*

It is easy to shoot—but not as Pope did. The shafts of his satire rise sublimely: no poet's verse ever mounted higher than that wonderful flight with which the "Dunciad" concludes . . . [quotes IV, 629–656].[1]

In these astonishing lines Pope reaches I think, to the very greatest height which his sublime art has attained, and shows himself the equal of all poets of all times. It is the brightest ardour, the loftiest assertion of truth, the most generous wisdom illustrated by the noblest poetic figure, and spoken in words the aptest, grandest, and most harmonious. It is heroic courage speaking: a splendid declaration of righteous wrath and war. It is the gage flung down, and the silver trumpet ringing defiance to falsehood and tyranny, deceit, dulness, superstition. It is Truth, the champion, shining and intrepid, and fronting the great world-tyrant with armies of slaves at his back. It is a wonderful and victorious single combat, in that great battle which has always been waging since society began.

In speaking of a work of consummate art one does not try to show what it actually is, for that were vain; but what it is like, and what are the sensations produced in the mind of him who views it. And in considering Pope's admirable career, I am forced into similitudes drawn from other courage and greatness, and into comparing him with those who achieved triumphs in actual war. I think of the works of young Pope as I do of the actions of young Bonaparte or young Nelson. In their common life you will find frailties and meannesses, as great as the vices and follies of the meanest men. But in the presence of the great occasion, the great soul flashes out, and conquers transcendent. In thinking of the splendour of Pope's young victories, of his merit, unequalled as his renown, I hail and salute the achieving genius, and do homage to the pen of a hero.

[1] "He (Johnson) repeats to us, in his forcible melodious manner, the concluding lines of the 'Dunciad.' "—*Boswell.* "Mr. Langton informed us that he once related to Johnson (on the authority of Spence), that Pope himself admired these lines so much that when he repeated them his voice faltered. 'And well it might, sir,' said Johnson, 'for they are noble lines.' "—*J. Boswell, junior.*

From "Prior, Gay, and Pope," *The English Humourists of the Eighteenth Century* (1853); reprinted from *The English Humourists, The Four Georges*, London, J. M. Dent & Sons Ltd. (Everyman's Library), 1929, pp. 179–181. (Editor's title.)

John Conington

Correctness, Homer, and Horace

THAT Pope is the most correct of English poets is a notion which of late years various eminent critics have been at considerable pains to explode. The opinion is one which has the advantage of prescription, having apparently been a received doctrine for many years after the poet's death. Yet, if a question can be decided by the authority of great names, it would seem necessary at once to abandon such a position. Hazlitt, in his "Lectures on the English Poets," mentions particular instances of incorrectness which are to be found in Pope; and an article in the "North British Review," for August 1848, attributed to Mr. de Quincey, analyses one or two passages in the poems at considerable length, with a view to prove that the belief, in which it is admitted that the poet himself shared, is a gross popular error. Lord Macaulay, in his "Essay on Byron," is equally strenuous on the same side, though the ground which he takes up is somewhat different. According to him, what Pope and the post-Restoration poets aimed at and realised was not real correctness, which, with him, is synonymous with excellence and truthfulness to nature, but the pseudo-correctness of conformity to an utterly artificial and illusory standard. It appears to me, however, that the old view was substantially a just one, that there is a legitimate and intelligible sense in which Pope may be said to have especially earned the praise of correctness, and that this praise discriminates him, not only from his predecessors, but also to some extent from subsequent poets. The ideal which he laboured to attain was a reasonable one, and his efforts were suffi-

ciently, though not wholly, successful. The question will, perhaps, be found to be partly a question of words; but the right understanding of it is, I think, important, if we wish really to appreciate the position which Pope occupies as a poet.

It is worthy of remark that, as the "North British" Reviewer admits, correctness is a thing on which Pope is known to have especially valued himself. He had scarcely commenced authorship when it was placed before him by one of his earliest critical friends as the principal object after which he was bound to strive. "Walsh," he told Spence, "used to encourage me much, and used to tell me that there was one way left of excelling; for, though we had several great poets, we never had any one great poet who was correct; and desired me to make that my study and aim." It is easy to smile at this criticism, and to ask what is the worth of a canon which thus summarily condemns Shakspeare, Spenser, and Milton as alike deficient in the particular requirement sought. These writers, it is now generally acknowledged, far transcend Pope in grandeur and comprehensiveness of conception; they have achieved triumphs of expression to which he was unequal, and struck chords of melody of which he never dreamed. Yet it is possible that he may have been conscious of something in himself which they had not, and possible, too, that this special acquirement may have been a thing of real and enduring value. That he and his contemporaries should have overrated it is only too likely; that they should have been altogether wrong in their estimate of its

From "The Poetry of Pope" (reprinted from *Oxford Essays*, 1858), *Miscellaneous Writings*, ed. J. A. Symonds, 2 vols., London, Longmans, Green, and Co., 1872, I, 1–73. (Editor's title.)

ge of poetry. "Which being done with
dy diligence," may remind us of the
saic style—half oratorical, half conver-
ional—in which Lucretius is apt to pass
om sentence to sentence. Altogether, the
ssage does not seem to conform to Cole-
dge's definition of poetry, which is at bot-
om much the same as the demand for cor-
ectness, "the *best* words in their right
places.". . .

On the whole, . . . Milton lived too
much in an atmosphere of his own, too little in sympathy with the generation in
which his greatest works were produced,
to impart to English poetry that correctness of which it was beginning to find its
need. He might have led it by a steeper and
more rugged way to a higher point of exaltation; but other guides were preferred,
and it was not till they had had their day
that his influence came to be really felt.
These writers were, as might be expected,
themselves incumbered more or less, especially at first, with the faults of carelessness and roughness, against which it is
their praise to have protested. As compared
with Pope, Dryden is certainly an incorrect
poet. He is full of inequalities—at one time
polished and vigorous, at another flat and
slovenly. Yet his felicities are of a kind
which can hardly have been attained without some use of the file, some conscious
imitation of classical models. As a prose
writer, he may perhaps be called the father
of English criticism; and it is not likely
that his practice should have been uninflu-
enced by his precepts. In his "Defence of
the Essay on Dramatic Poesy," he says of
himself,

As for the more material faults of writing which
are properly mine, though I see many of them, I
want leisure to amend them. It is enough for
those who make one poem the business of their
lives to leave that correct; yet, excepting Virgil,
I never met with any which was so in any language.

It is of this spirit of criticism that Pope's
poetry is the triumphant embodiment. He

appears to have been the first English writer possessed of high poetical power (Milton I have already intimated that I should
wish to except) who addressed himself to
the composition of poetry with the full de-
termination to do his best. He occasionally
published poems which he afterwards
found himself able to improve; that, so far
from proving that he acquiesced in imper-
fection, is really an evidence to the contrary: but we may be sure that he never
published his first draft. Even in his most
finished pieces there may be occasionally
something that more study might have
mended—an ill-turned thought, an inaccu-
rate expression, a bad rhyme. So much may
be readily conceded to those who, like Hazlitt and Mr. de Quincey, think the praise of
his correctness exaggerated. But are there
no blemishes of a similar kind in writers
who are commonly allowed in these respects to come little short of perfection—
in Virgil or Horace, for example? The
point is not that Pope was universally correct, but that correctness, in the sense in
which I have attempted to explain it, was
at any rate one of his leading characteristics, and that the instances of carelessness
which can be quoted from his works are
not sufficiently numerous or important to
disturb the general impression. Nor do I
think it can be maintained that such a
praise is slight or nugatory. It is the praise
which is given to a schoolboy for a good
exercise; but it goes along also with that
schooling to which a wise man will be willing to submit all his life. If we ignore it,
we must ignore nearly the whole of what
criticism has done for literary composition
from the days of Horace downwards. . . .

The writers who succeeded Pope attempted to pursue the same course of refinement, but they had not the same true in-
stinct to guide them, and the material
which they strove to elaborate gave way
under their hands. They either repeated
the more obvious features of his language
and his rhythm, or, in endeavouring to
improve upon them, ran into that excess

nature and importance is far from probable.

Perhaps there is no better help towards a true apprehension of the English poetry of the eighteenth century than a knowledge of the poetry of Augustan Rome. The similarity of the two periods, as phases of national literature, has often been pointed out: it would be easy, if this were the case, to pursue the parallel into detail. Now it is curious that what Walsh said to Pope is precisely the same as what Horace said to his countrymen. He tells them, almost in so many words, that, though they had had several great poets, they never had any one great poet who was correct. . . . What it was that Horace quarrelled with in the poetry of his predecessors . . . was, in short, that they did not spend sufficient pains upon their poetry; that they did not make it as good as they might have done. Their treatment of a subject was not sufficiently varied; their language was not sufficiently elegant; their versification was not sufficiently polished. . . .

Even Shakspeare, if we analyse him calmly, cannot be said to have the characteristics of a finished writer. It is true that his obedience to the eternal laws of truth and beauty was infinitely more comprehensive in its range, infinitely higher in its quality, than Pope's. But it is no less true that there are rules of style and versification, not arbitrary, but grounded on those very laws, which Shakspeare neglected and Pope observed. We know, in fact, that Shakspeare's habits of composition were unfavourable to the attainment of that faultless propriety which is the reward of long-continued labour. Pope, as was to be expected, has noted this in his imitation of . . . [a passage from Horace] :—

Otway failed to polish or refine,
And fluent Shakspeare scarce effaced a line:
E'en copious Dryden wanted, or forgot,
That last and greatest art, the art to blot.

What is to be said of such expressions as "*reverbs* no hollowness," "*exsufflicate* and

blowed surmises," whe[...]
in contempt of analog[...]
when Lucretius talks of *a*[...]
entia, pestilitas for *pestil*[...]
to the passages where Shak[...]
may properly be brought i[...]
the rhyming couplets in the[...]
nor poems, and the sonnets, [...]
tained that there is no wea[...]
dundance, such as might have[...]
ed by an exacting self-criticism[...]
stanza of the "Rape of Lucrece[...]
an instance of what I mean :—

When they had sworn to this advised[...]
They did conclude to bear dead Lucre[...]
To show her bleeding body thorough [...]
And so to publish Tarquin's foul offen[...]
Which being done with speedy diligen[...]
   The Romans plausibly did give consen[...]
   To Tarquin's everlasting banishment.

This is, of course, no fair specimen of [...]
beauties of the poem; but even were[...]
more exceptional than it is, it would st[...]
illustrate the proposition that its author [...]
frequently unequal to himself. There is[...]
something not ineffective in the monotony
of the lines and the simplicity of the expression; but it can hardly be doubted
that the one might have been varied and
the other rendered less prosaic, without
striking a note out of harmony with the
natural conclusion of a story so melancholy. "*Did* conclude," "*did* give consent,"
were too common in Shakespeare's time to
offend a critical reader; but Pope surely
did good service in expelling them, by precept and ridicule,[1] from the ordinary lan-

[1] "Another nicety is in relation to expletives,
whether words or syllables, which are made use
of purely to supply a vacancy. *Do*, before verbs
plural, is absolutely such, and it is not improbable
that future refiners may explode *did* and *does* in
the same manner, which are almost always used
for the sake of rhyme." (Pope to Walsh—Bowles,
vol. vii. p. 75.) So the well-known "Expletives
their feeble aid do join," of the *Essay on Criticism*. The ridicule of expletives, like that of the
lines of ten monosyllables, is taken from a passage
in Dryden's *Essay on Dramatic Poesy*, as Malone
remarks; the expletives, however, which Dryden
singles out for censure are "for to," and "unto."

which it was the very object of his chastened taste to restrain. A spirit of reaction became apparent: Churchill endeavoured to return to the negligent vigour of Dryden; Cowper, Churchill's schoolfellow and admirer, went further, not only making the heroic couplet less mellifluous, but reviving the fashion of blank-verse writing, which he learned to use as it had not been used by Thomson or Young; till at last the springs of new life in taste and opinion which arose in the great political convulsion of those days burst up to the surface, and the literary traditions of a century and a half were submerged or swept away. Since then it may be almost said that correctness such as Pope's is to be numbered among the lost arts; the leaders of the revolution, like Coleridge, Wordsworth, and Keats, disdained it as the badge of an unimaginative and artificial school; the Conservatives, like Rogers and Campbell, were scarcely strong enough to realise in practice what they upheld in theory; while Byron, who, as Lord Macaulay happily remarks, belonged to both parties, not by turns but simultaneously, bears probably more marks of slovenliness and haste than any great poet of the time. But the importance of form in poetry is not a doctrine which can long be lost sight of while any feeling for art survives; and though the circumstantial differences between Mr. Tennyson and Pope are too many and too great to justify any parallel of the one with the other, we may rejoice in the possession of a writer whose self-criticism is as exacting as Pope's own, and who has taught us once more that high poetry will not lightly tolerate a trivial phrase or a tuneless line. . . .

To censure Pope's "Homer" as un-Homeric has now become a cheap and easy task. It was always known not to be a close rendering of the original; and the difference of centuries between the manner of the pre-historic age of Greek literature and the manner of the English poetry of Queen Anne's reign has at last made itself felt by readers of every sort. Whatever errors there may be in the conceptions of style which prevail in the present day, there can be no doubt that a keen appreciation of the characteristic style of different periods, a perception of the historical analogies of different manners of writing, are more generally diffused now than was the case even thirty years ago. The various translators of Homer, as a general rule, have simply rendered him into the style in which they were themselves accustomed to write—some with greater, some with less fidelity to the words of the Greek, but none of them paying any special attention to the Homeric manner. Chapman's early English fortunately happens to coincide to some extent with Homer's early Greek; but though his simplicity strikes us in contrast with the conventional art of a modern poet, he is an Elizabethan writer all over, continually running off into quaint conceits, forced metaphors, and a philosophical jargon, for which it is needless to say that his author affords no warrant. Ogilby and Hobbes simply fashioned "Homer" into such English as they could command; and if their language is mean and their metre rugged, it is because they had not the genius or the skill to do better. Dryden, indeed, in the preface to his "Fables," dwells at some length on the difference between Homer and Virgil, asserting that the former is more congenial to his own temperament, and consequently more pleasant to translate, than the latter; but his general notion is that Homer is more rapid and careless, Virgil more slow and careful; and he shows his sense of the distinction when he passes from one to the other, simply by throwing off restraint, disdaining to correct his language, and taking liberties with versification: he imitates the simplicity of the old Greek garb merely by appearing in public in his own dressing-gown and slippers. Cowper, writing after Pope, had the advantage of knowing what to avoid; but he was misled by a false analogy, and seeing in Milton a great epic poet, austere in his manner and repellent of meretricious ornament, attempted to force on Homer a style which, rightly considered, is almost as artificial as Virgil's, and which, moreover, he was himself unequal to wield. . . .

So much it was necessary to say on the theory of translation; and now we are free to do justice to the extraordinary and unrivalled excellence of the poem, as a product of Pope's peculiar power. Probably no other work of his has had so much influence on the national taste and feeling for poetry. It has been—I hope it is still—the delight of every intelligent schoolboy: they read "of kings, and heroes, and of mighty deeds," in language which, in its calm majestic flow, unhasting, unresting, carries them on as irresistibly as Homer's own could do, were they born readers of Greek; and their minds are filled with a conception of the heroic age, not indeed strictly true, but almost as near the truth as that which was entertained by Virgil himself. Their imagination is refined, exalted, satisfied. All the felicities of Pope's higher style are concentrated in this translation. It occupied ten of the best years of his life, and it adequately represents the fruits which powers like his were sure to produce by the mere force of constant exercise. The peculiarities of his own mind, which sometimes offend us when exhibited on a small scale, do not appear equally unpleasing when we see them more at large. It may be only an arbitrary fancy, but I do not find the modernisation of Homer nearly so frigid as the modernisation of Chaucer. The language which Achilles and Agamemnon are made to talk seems less inappropriate than the words which are put into the mouth of Eloisa. One cause doubtless is, that Pope was compelled to allow himself less latitude and exhibit himself less. His "Homer," though a sufficiently free translation, is a translation after all. It was on this limited neutral ground, I incline to think, that his genius as a writer on heroic or ideal subjects was best qualified to expatiate. For such themes it was well that

others should find the thoughts, he undertaking to supply the manner, the diction, and the numbers. . . .

Dryden, as was just now observed, from his incredible carelessness and rashness, fails just where he might have been expected to succeed; he sees that factitious dignity is no longer required, and therefore takes out a license to be vulgar; and in the very same volume, where he shows, in his adaptations of Chaucer and Boccaccio, how well he could write while on his good behaviour, Jupiter is made to call Juno his "household curse," his "lawful plague," his "other squinting eye"; and the gods are sent off to bed "drunken and drowsy," even the Thunderer applying "his swimming head to needful sleep." Tickell's version of the First Book of the "Iliad," which appeared within a day or two of Pope's, and was the cause of the rupture with Addison, though hailed by the Whig coterie as "the best that ever was made," is really a performance of no remarkable merit; a respectable production of the Addisonian school, with far less vigour than Dryden's, and far less splendour than Pope's; and the passages in which, as his friend Young told him, he was allowed even by partial judges to have outdone his rival, can only be called inferior, though meritorious, specimens of the heroic style of which that rival proved himself so great a master. There is another translation of the greater part of the First Book, by Maynwaring. . . . Pope, while smarting under the non-recognition of his own superiority, had thoughts of republishing this version, together with Dryden's and Tickell's, side by side with his own, that the public might judge more readily of their respective merits. Let us do him some portion of that justice which booksellers' difficulties prevented him from doing to himself, by setting down in juxtaposition a short passage from each of the four translations. The specimens I have selected are, so far as I can judge, adequate representatives of the average quality of each; though Dryden in particular, along with some worse passages, contains some better. Those who care to compare them with the Greek, which is not my present object, may turn to "Iliad," i. vv. 233–247.

DRYDEN.

But by this sceptre solemnly I swear
(Which never more green leaf or growing branch shall bear,
Torn from the tree, and given by Jove to those
Who laws dispense and mighty wrongs oppose),
That when the Grecians want my wonted aid,
No gift shall bribe it, and no prayer persuade.
When Hector comes, the homicide, to wield
His conquering arms, with corps to strew the field,
Then shalt thou mourn thy pride, and late confess
Thy wrong repented, when 'tis past redress.
  He said, and with disdain, in open view,
Against the ground his golden sceptre threw;
Then sate: with boiling rage Atrides burned,
And foam betwixt his gnashing grinders churned.

MAYNWARING.

But by this awful sceptre now I swear
(Which ne'er again will happy branches bear,
Nor native bark, nor growing leaves will shoot,
But left on distant hills the kindly root,
And now with Grecian judges must remain,
Who right dispense, and sacred laws maintain),
Hear what I swear: whene'er the Greeks shall want
My needful aid, destruction to prevent,
And with regret their lost Achilles mourn,
No prayers nor gifts shall bribe me to return:
Hector shall strew with slaughtered foes the field,
And no relief thy impotence shall yield;
But, torn with deep remorse, thy heart shall break
For wronging thus in arms the bravest Greek.
  The speech concluded, in disdain he tossed
His sceptre down, with golden studs embossed:
Atrides also stormed.

TICKELL.

But thou my fixed, my final purpose hear:
By this dread sceptre solemnly I swear,
By this (which, once from out the forest torn,
Nor leaf nor shade shall ever more adorn,
Which never more its verdure must renew,
Lopped from the vital stem whence first it grew,
But given by Jove the sons of men to awe,
Now sways the nations and confirms the law),
A day shall come when for this hour's disdain
The Greeks shall wish for me, and wish in vain;
Nor thou, though grieved, the wanted aid afford,
When heaps on heaps shall fall by Hector's sword:
Too late with anguish shall thy heart be torn
That the first Greek was made the public scorn.
  He said, and mounting with a furious bound,
He dashed his studded sceptre on the ground;
Then sat: Atrides, eager to reply,
On the fierce champion glanced a vengeful eye.

POPE.

Now by this sacred sceptre hear me swear,
Which never more shall leaves or blossoms bear,
Which, severed from the trunk (as I from thee),
On the bare mountains left its parent tree;
This sceptre, formed by tempered steel to prove
An ensign of the delegates of Jove,
From whom the power of laws and justice springs
(Tremendous oath! inviolate to kings):
By this I swear, when bleeding Greece again
Shall call Achilles, she shall call in vain.
When, flushed with slaughter, Hector comes to spread
The purpled shore with mountains of the dead,
Then shalt thou mourn the affront thy madness gave,
Forced to deplore, when impotent to save:
Then rage in bitterness of soul, to know
This act has made the bravest Greek thy foe.
  He spoke, and furious hurled against the ground
His sceptre, starred with golden studs around:
Then sternly silent sat. With like disdain
The raging king returned his frowns again.

This will enable us to measure Pope's superiority to his predecessors. What they did with more or less success, he did excellently. Dryden was the only one of them that could have stood the competition with him; and Dryden was exposed to defeat by his own disdainful security. Pope's lines are, indeed, a memorable comment on what was urged in the early part of this es-

say about the exactingness of his self-criticism. We feel that the passage could not
have been written at once—that his first
thoughts must have more nearly resembled
those of his competitors, and that it can
have been only after many reconsidera-
tions that they assumed their present form.
I do not know what evidence would be furnished by the famous MS. of Pope's "Iliad" in the British Museum, which I have
never had the opportunity of consulting;
but the specimens of other passages quoted
by Johnson and by Disraeli the elder are
enough to show what it probably would be;
and we must not forget that there are such
things as mental erasures, effacing first
draughts, which have never been written
down.[2]

Perhaps there will be no more conven-
ient place than the present for speaking of
the epic poem, which was the project of
Pope's latest years. He told Spence that he
should certainly have written an epic poem
if he had not engaged in the translation of
Homer, so that it is perhaps to that cause
that we owe the non-fulfilment of a dream
which actually took substance in his early
boyhood, and towards the end of his life
was regarded as a thing half accomplished
already. . . . It was Pope's happiness,
when still meditating epic song, to find
himself condemned "ten years to comment
and translate.". . . Pope was, in fact, re-
alising his own dream without knowing it,
in a better way than if he had worked on
his own plan. His greater epics are the English "Iliad" and "Odyssey," as his lesser
are the "Rape of the Lock" and the "Dunciad.". . .

Pope's predilection for ethical poetry
grew on him, as I have said, in his later
life. In his last illness he compared himself
to Socrates, dispensing his morality among
his friends just as he was dying. His last
compositions, however, were rather satiric

than strictly ethical. But satire and ethics
had come to be associated in his mind as
two aspects of the same thing. Even the
ferocity of the "Dunciad" he wished to be
regarded as virtuous indignation, the natural feeling of one whose life was a "more
endearing song" than his poetry, against
scribblers, who had not only wounded his
taste by their dulness and his just self-love
by their unprovoked libels, but outraged
his moral sense by the scandalousness of
their lives. On the other hand, the exordium of the "Essay on Man," with its sport-
ing metaphors of "shooting folly as it
flies," and "catching manners living as
they rise," and its proposal "to laugh
where we must," and "be candid where we
can," promises us satire as well as ethics.
Again, in the "New Dunciad," the last substantive work which he seems to have written, he uses up materials which had been
intended to appear in a new series of "Moral Epistles." His "Imitations of Horace," of
which it now remains to speak, extend over
several years. . . . Like the "Essay on
Man," they were suggested to him by Bolingbroke, and the suggestion was this time
an eminently fortunate one. The thought of
pointing an ancient satire with modern applications had occurred to others. . . .
But Pope's imitations, it is needless to say,
are so excellent of their kind as to obscure
all previous attempts, and constitute, as it
were, a class by themselves. As in the translation of Homer, he has the advantage of
being able to superadd his own terseness
and brilliancy to Horace's sense, while he
can afford to allow himself more freedom,
and keep with safety at a greater distance
from an original whose genius and literary
position were in many respects nearly akin
to his own. Johnson, perhaps, thinking of
his own "Juvenal," and writing in one of
those gloomy fits of self-depreciation of
which we have a specimen in the opening
of the celebrated preface to the "English
Dictionary," observes that "such imitations" as Pope's "cannot give pleasure to

---

[2] "One must tune each line over in one's head, to
try whether they go right or not."—Pope, speaking
of pastoral versification (Malone's *Spence*, p. 72).

common readers: the man of learning may be sometimes surprised and delighted by an unexpected parallel; but the comparison requires knowledge of the original, which will likewise often detect strained applications." Yet I am mistaken if a common reader may not enjoy these imitations nearly as much as any of Pope's more original satires—if they have not, in fact, yielded nearly as large a percentage of familiar quotations; while those who read Horace certainly have the additional pleasure of seeing how dexterously the English poet pursues the track of the Latin, now striking out a happy translation, now an unexpected analogy, sometimes deviating from the way, but never losing it. We have none of those elaborate characters in the delineation of which Pope shone so much; but there is the same power of touching contemporary events gracefully, the same nod of easy recognition for a passing friend, the same transient flush as an opponent crosses his path, while the texture of the whole poem is generally stronger than what Pope cares to employ in his own occasional pieces. They are like a felicitous quotation, which is often worth more than an independent *bon mot,* having all its own wit and wisdom, and all the associations of the original passage besides. The one point in which Pope differs most markedly from Horace is his versification. It has been

said [3] that the Roman poet wilfully untuned his harp when he commenced satirist; Pope, without attempting to import into satire the sonorous cadence of the epic, polishes and points the lines which are to reproduce Horace as scrupulously as those which are to render Homer. It is what Roman satire would have been had it accepted the regulating mechanism of the elegiac couplet—an epigram, as one of the writers in the Greek anthology expresses it, prolonged into a rhapsody. Each form has its advantage for what is, in fact, an embodiment of sparkling social talk, witty and wise—the loose fireside robe as well as the trim evening dress—and we need not adjust their claims to preference. . . .

But it is time to conclude a task which it is perhaps presumptuous to have undertaken. I should be glad to think that what has been here attempted insufficiently would be adequately performed by some other writer. Pope's poetry has hardly received yet the careful critical examination which it deserves. The last century, indeed, can boast of Johnson's masterly critique, and the more elaborate, though less penetrating, survey by Warton. But I am not aware of anything in our own day which meets the requirements of the subject.

[3] The expression is quoted by Scott—*Life of Dryden,* p. 239 (ed. 1834)—but I do not know where it is to be met with.

Matthew Arnold

Pope's Translation of Homer

I CONSIDER that when Bentley said of Pope's translation, "It was a pretty poem, but must not be called Homer," the work, in spite of all its power and attractiveness, was judged. . . .

It is in vain that Cowper insists on his fidelity: "my chief boast is that I have adhered closely to my original":—"the matter found in me, whether the reader like it or not, is found also in Homer; and the matter not found in me, how much soever the reader may admire it, is found only in Mr. Pope." To suppose that it is *fidelity* to an original to give its matter, unless you at the same time give its manner; or, rather, to suppose that you can really give its matter at all, unless you can give its manner, is just the mistake of our pre-Raphaelite school of painters, who do not understand that the peculiar effect of nature resides in the whole and not in the parts. So the peculiar effect of a poet resides in his manner and movement, not in his words taken separately. It is well known how conscientiously literal is Cowper in his translation of Homer. It is well known how extravagantly free is Pope.

"So let it be!
Portents and prodigies are lost on me":

that is Pope's rendering of the words,

Ξάνθε, τί μοι θάνατον μαντεύεαι; οὐδέ τί σε χρή.[1]
"Xanthus, why prophesiest thou my death to me? thou needest not at all":—

yet, on the whole, Pope's translation of the *Iliad* is more Homeric than Cowper's, for it is more rapid.

[1] *Iliad*, xix. 420.

Pope's movement, however, though rapid, is not of the same kind as Homer's; and here I come to the real objection to rhyme in a translation of Homer. It is commonly said that rhyme is to be abandoned in a translation of Homer, because "the exigencies of rhyme," to quote Mr. Newman, "positively forbid faithfulness"; because "a just translation of any ancient poet in rhyme," to quote Cowper, "is impossible." This, however, is merely an accidental objection to rhyme. If this were all, it might be supposed, that if rhymes were more abundant, Homer could be adequately translated in rhyme. But this is not so; there is a deeper, a substantial objection to rhyme in a translation of Homer. It is, that rhyme inevitably tends to pair lines which in the original are independent, and thus the movement of the poem is changed. . . .

Rhyme certainly, by intensifying antithesis, can intensify separation, and this is precisely what Pope does; but this balanced rhetorical antithesis, though very effective, is entirely un-Homeric. And this is what I mean by saying that Pope fails to render Homer, because he does not render his plainness and directness of style and diction. Where Homer marks separation by moving away, Pope marks it by antithesis. No passage could show this better than [Sarpedon's speech to Glaucus, in the twelfth book of the *Iliad*]. . . .

The passage is just one of those in translating which Pope will be at his best, a passage of strong emotion and oratorical movement, not of simple narrative or description.

From *On Translating Homer* (1861) ; reprinted from *On the Study of Celtic Literature and On Translating Homer*, New York, Macmillan and Co., 1883, pp. 144–160. (Editor's title.)

Pope translates the passage thus:—

"Could all our care elude the gloomy grave
Which claims no less the fearful than the brave,
For lust of fame I should not vainly dare
In fighting fields, nor urge thy soul to war:
But since, alas! ignoble age must come,
Disease, and death's inexorable doom;
The life which others pay, let us bestow,
And give to fame what we to nature owe."

Nothing could better exhibit Pope's prodigious talent; and nothing, too, could be better in its own way. But, as Bentley said, "You must not call it Homer." One feels that Homer's thought has passed through a literary and rhetorical crucible, and come out highly intellectualised; come out in a form which strongly impresses us, indeed, but which no longer impresses us in the same way as when it was uttered by Homer. The antithesis of the last two lines—

The life which others pay, let us bestow,
And give to fame what we to nature owe"—

is excellent, and is just suited to Pope's heroic couplet; but neither the antithesis itself, nor the couplet which conveys it, is suited to the feeling or to the movement of the Homeric ἴομεν.

A literary and intellectualised language is, however, in its own way well suited to grand matters; and Pope, with a language of this kind and his own admirable talent, comes off well enough as long as he has passion, or oratory, or a great crisis to deal with. Even here, as I have been pointing out, he does not render Homer; but he and his style are in themselves strong. It is when he comes to level passages, passages of narrative or description, that he and his style are sorely tried, and prove themselves weak. A perfectly plain direct style can of course convey the simplest matter as naturally as the grandest; indeed, it must be harder for it, one would say, to convey a grand matter worthily and nobly, than to convey a common matter, as alone such a matter should be conveyed, plainly and simply. But the style of Rasselas is incomparably better fitted to describe a sage philosophising than a soldier lighting his campfire. The style of Pope is not the style of Rasselas; but it is equally a literary style, equally unfitted to describe a simple matter with the plain naturalness of Homer.

Every one knows the passage at the end of the eighth book of the *Iliad*, where the fires of the Trojan encampment are likened to the stars. It is very far from my wish to hold Pope up to ridicule, so I shall not quote the commencement of the passage, which in the original is of great and celebrated beauty, and in translating which Pope has been singularly and notoriously fortunate. But the latter part of the passage, where Homer leaves the stars, and comes to the Trojan fires, treats of the plainest, most matter-of-fact subject possible, and deals with this, as Homer always deals with every subject, in the plainest and most straightforward style. "So many in number, between the ships and the streams of Xanthus, shone forth in front of Troy the fires kindled by the Trojans. There were kindled a thousand fires in the plain; and by each one there sat fifty men in the light of the blazing fire. And the horses, munching white barley and rye, and standing by the chariots, waited for the bright-throned Morning." [2]

In Pope's translation, this plain story becomes the following:—

"So many flames before proud Ilion blaze,
And brighten glimmering Xanthus with their
    rays;
The long reflections of the distant fires
Gleam on the walls, and tremble on the spires.
A thousand piles the dusky horrors gild,
And shoot a shady lustre o'er the field.
Full fifty guards each flaming pile attend,
Whose umbered arms, by fits, thick flashes
    send;
Loud neigh the coursers o'er their heaps of
    corn,
And ardent warriors wait the rising morn."

It is for passages of this sort, which, after all, form the bulk of a narrative poem, that

[2] *Iliad*, viii. 560.

Pope's style is so bad. In elevated passages he is powerful, as Homer is powerful, though not in the same way; but in plain narrative, where Homer is still power and delightful, Pope, by the inherent fault of his style, is ineffective and out of taste. Wordsworth says somewhere, that wherever Virgil seems to have composed "with his eye on the object," Dryden fails to render him. Homer invariably composes "with his eye on the object," whether the object be a moral or a material one: Pope composes with his eye on his style, into which he translates his object, whatever it is. That, therefore, which Homer conveys to us immediately, Pope conveys to us through a medium. He aims at turning Homer's sentiments pointedly and rhetorically; at investing Homer's description with ornament and dignity. A sentiment may be changed by being put into a pointed and oratorical form, yet may still be very effective in that form; but a description, the moment it takes its eyes off that which it is to describe, and begins to think of ornamenting itself, is worthless.

Therefore, I say, the translator of Homer should penetrate himself with a sense of the plainness and directness of Homer's style; of the simplicity with which Homer's thought is evolved and expressed. He has Pope's fate before his eyes, to show him what a divorce may be created even between the most gifted translator and Homer by an artificial evolution of thought and a literary cast of style.

Dryden and Pope: Classics of Our Prose

THE age of Dryden, together with our whole eighteenth century which followed it, sincerely believed itself to have produced poetical classics of its own, and even to have made advance, in poetry, beyond all its predecessors. Dryden regards as not seriously disputable the opinion "that the sweetness of English verse was never understood or practised by our fathers." Cowley could see nothing at all in Chaucer's poetry. Dryden heartily admired it, and, as we have seen, praised its matter admirably; but of its exquisite manner and movement all he can find to say is that "there is the rude sweetness of a Scotch tune in it, which is natural and pleasing, though not perfect." Addison, wishing to praise Chaucer's numbers, compares them with Dryden's own. And all through the eighteenth century, and down even into our own times, the stereotyped phrase of approbation for good verse found in our early poetry has been, that it even approached the verse of Dryden, Addison, Pope, and Johnson.

Are Dryden and Pope poetical classics? Is the historic estimate, which represents them as such, and which has been so long established that it cannot easily give way, the real estimate? Wordsworth and Coleridge, as is well known, denied it; but the authority of Wordsworth and Coleridge does not weigh much with the young generation, and there are many signs to show that the eighteenth century and its judgments are coming into favour again. Are the favourite poets of the eighteenth century classics?

It is impossible within my present limits to discuss the question fully. And what man of letters would not shrink from seeming to dispose dictatorially of the claims of two men who are, at any rate, such masters in letters as Dryden and

From "The Study of Poetry" (1880); reprinted from *Essays in Criticism*, Second Series, London, Macmillan and Co., 1898, pp. 35–42. (Editor's title.)

Pope; two men of such admirable talent, both of them, and one of them, Dryden, a man, on all sides, of such energetic and genial power? And yet, if we are to gain the full benefit from poetry, we must have the real estimate of it. I cast about for some mode of arriving, in the present case, at such an estimate without offence. And perhaps the best way is to begin, as it is easy to begin, with cordial praise.

When we find Chapman, the Elizabethan translator of Homer, expressing himself in his preface thus: "Though truth in her very nakedness sits in so deep a pit, that from Gades to Aurora and Ganges few eyes can sound her, I hope yet those few here will so discover and confirm that, the date being out of her darkness in this morning of our poet, he shall now gird his temples with the sun,"—we pronounce that such a prose is intolerable. When we find Milton writing: "And long it was not after, when I was confirmed in this opinion, that he, who would not be frustrate of his hope to write well hereafter in laudable things, ought himself to be a true poem,"—we pronounce that such a prose has its own grandeur, but that it is obsolete and inconvenient. But when we find Dryden telling us: "What Virgil wrote in the vigour of his age, in plenty and at ease, I have undertaken to translate in my declining years; struggling with wants, oppressed with sickness, curbed in my genius, liable to be misconstrued in all I write,"—then we exclaim that here at last we have the true English prose, a prose such as we would all gladly use if we only knew how. Yet Dryden was Milton's contemporary.

But after the Restoration the time had come when our nation felt the imperious need of a fit prose. So, too, the time had likewise come when our nation felt the imperious need of freeing itself from the absorbing preoccupation which religion in the Puritan age had exercised. It was impossible that this freedom should be brought about without some negative excess, without some neglect and impairment of the religious life of the soul; and the spiritual history of the eighteenth century shows us that the freedom was not achieved without them. Still, the freedom was achieved; the preoccupation, an undoubtedly baneful and retarding one if it had continued, was got rid of. And as with religion amongst us at that period, so it was also with letters. A fit prose was a necessity; but it was impossible that a fit prose should establish itself amongst us without some touch of frost to the imaginative life of the soul. The needful qualities for a fit prose are regularity, uniformity, precision, balance. The men of letters, whose destiny it may be to bring their nation to the attainment of a fit prose, must of necessity, whether they work in prose or in verse, give a predominating, an almost exclusive attention to the qualities of regularity, uniformity, precision, balance. But an almost exclusive attention to these qualities involves some repression and silencing of poetry.

We are to regard Dryden as the puissant and glorious founder, Pope as the splendid high priest, of our age of prose and reason, of our excellent and indispensable eighteenth century. For the purposes of their mission and destiny their poetry, like their prose, is admirable. Do you ask me whether Dryden's verse, take it almost where you will, is not good?

"A milk-white Hind, immortal and unchanged,
Fed on the lawns and in the forest ranged."

I answer: Admirable for the purposes of the inaugurator of an age of prose and reason. Do you ask me whether Pope's verse, take it almost where you will, is not good?

"To Hounslow Heath I point, and Banstead Down;
Thence comes your mutton, and these chicks my own."

I answer: Admirable for the purposes of the high priest of an age of prose and reason. But do you ask me whether such verse proceeds from men with an adequate poetic criticism of life, from men whose criticism of life has a high seriousness, or even, without that high seriousness, has poetic largeness, freedom, insight, benignity? Do you ask me whether the application of ideas to life in the verse of these men, often a powerful application, no doubt, is a powerful *poetic* application? Do you ask me whether the poetry of these men has either the matter or the inseparable manner of such an adequate poetic criticism; whether it has the accent of

"Absent thee from felicity awhile . . ."

or of

"And what is else not to be overcome . . ."

or of

"O martyr souded in virginitee!"

I answer: It has not and cannot have them; it is the poetry of the builders of an age of prose and reason. Though they may write in verse, though they may in a certain sense be masters of the art of versification, Dryden and Pope are not classics of our poetry, they are classics of our prose.

Poetry Conceived in the Soul

THE difference between genuine poetry and the poetry of Dryden, Pope, and all their school, is briefly this: their poetry is conceived and composed in their wits, genuine poetry is conceived and composed in the soul. The difference between the two kinds of poetry is immense. They differ profoundly in their modes of language, they differ profoundly in their modes of evolution. The poetic language of our eighteenth century in general is the language of men composing *without their eye on the object,* as Wordsworth excellently said of Dryden; language merely recalling the object, as the common language of prose does, and then dressing it out with a certain smartness and brilliancy for the fancy and understanding. This is called "splendid diction." The evolution of the poetry of our eighteenth century is likewise intellectual; it proceeds by ratiocination, antithesis, ingenious turns and conceits. This poetry is often eloquent, and always, in the hands of such masters as Dryden and Pope, clever; but it does not take us much below the surface of things, it does not give us the emotion of seeing things in their truth and beauty. The language of genuine poetry, on the other hand, is the language of one composing with his eye on the object; its evolution is that of a thing which has been plunged in the poet's soul until it comes forth naturally and necessarily. This sort of evolution is infinitely simpler than the other, and infinitely more satisfying; the same thing is true of the genuine poetic language likewise. But they are both of them also infinitely harder of attainment; they come only from those who, as Emerson says, "live from a great depth of being."

From "Thomas Gray" (1880); ibid., pp. 95–97. (Editor's title.)

Algernon Charles Swinburne

Pope's Heroic Spirit

AND what a spirit it was! how fiery bright and dauntless! . . . It rouses the blood, it kindles the heart, to remember what an indomitable force of heroic spirit, and sleepless always as fire, was inclosed in the pitiful body of the misshapen weakling whose whole life was spent in fighting the good fight of sense against folly, of light against darkness, of human speech against brute silence, of truth and reason and manhood against all the banded bestialities of all dunces and all dastards, all blackguardly blockheads and all blockheaded blackguards, who then as now were misbegotten by malignity or dulness.

From "A Century of English Poetry," *Fortnightly Review,* N.S. XXVIII (October 1880), 427. (Editor's title.)

William Paton Ker

Pope's Living Variety

FOR many years past, ever since the publication of Joseph Warton's *Essay on the Writings and Genius of Pope,* the poetry of Pope has been judged indirectly and with deference to opinions, cavils, and misgivings about him; even Dr. Johnson does not ignore "the question that has been put," whether Pope is a poet. Warton's Essay, the controversies of Bowles and Bryon, are apt to come between the reader and his author. Pope is valued not exactly as he is, but as he is thought about. . . .

Who doubts that the *Rape of the Lock* is Pope's most perfect work? It is one of the few things wholly without a flaw: is it vain and futile to ask where the music comes from and what it is worth with all its perfection?

It is not easy to understand without some pieces of ancient learning. There is pedantry in it, or what seems so to us who do not take the Heroic Poem as seriously as Milton, Dryden, and Pope; and unless you think seriously about the Epic, the Heroic Poem, you cannot think rightly of the *Rape of the Lock,* an Heroi-Comical Poem. This descriptive epithet is part of the tradition: it is used by Tassoni and Boileau. Pope was haunted by the orthodox critical doctrine of the Epic Poem. Like Milton and Dryden, he had the epic ambition; he wrote *Alcander Prince of Rhodes* when he was a boy; he made the plan of *Brutus,* an epic, when he was older. He saw the absurdity of the formalists such as the Reverend Father Le Bossu; he wrote for Steele's *Guardian* the comic receipt to make an epic poem which was incorporated in Martinus Scriblerus on the Art of Sinking in Poetry. But

his preface to the *Iliad* goes over, seriously, the same divisions of the subject: Fable, Characters, Machines, Allegory. His plan of *Brutus* follows the receipt; the fable is taken from Geoffrey of Monmouth, the machines are guardian angels of kingdoms, such as Dryden had recommended. He puts the old allegories into his Homer. The revised version of the *Rape of the Lock,* the very successful "machinery" of sylphs and gnomes, is something more than play; it is parody of one of the most important things in life for Pope, and his heroi-comical expedient, his most excellent lively burlesque substitute for the Olympians of Homer, is valued by him for its epic quality and its faithfulness to the epic idea. Pope makes his story out of no elements that are ungraceful; he aims at beauty, and the *Rape of the Lock,* a poem with no substance at all, is nothing but grace; the astral body of an heroic poem, pure form, an echo of divine music, how thin and clear!

This heroi-comical poem, if it is his finest and most absolute work, still does not fully give all his range, all his power: and Pope himself did not reckon it as letting him off the task of true heroic poetry. He went on to Homer; the first volume published in 1715 gives his opinion in the Preface: fifteen years after Dryden's Preface to his Fables and no less remarkable for its freedom of speech and its unlikeness to the poetry which it precedes. Both Dryden and Pope in their prose say things which their verse cannot say, and declare themselves, express themselves, more freely. Dryden's comparison of Chaucer and Ovid tells you more of Dryden's mind and tem-

From "Pope" (1921), *The Art of Poetry: Seven Lectures, 1920–1922,* Oxford, Clarendon Press, 1923, pp. 93–115. Reprinted by permission of the publisher. (Editor's title.)

per than his paraphrase of the Knight's Tale; Pope's description of Homer tells you something of Pope which you do not find explicitly in his verse. Here let me say with the greatest respect for Matthew Arnold that his description of Dryden and Pope as "classics of our prose" is a double sin in criticism, because it confuses the kinds in two ways; ignoring their poetry and their prose alike. For of course they are classics of our prose, when they write prose. Pope as a prose writer comes between Dryden and Johnson, less large in his periods than the older man, less formal than the younger. All three have the same strength of admiration, the same glorious delight when they meet with great poets. And this is Pope's theory of Homer. [Quotes third paragraph of Preface, on Homer's "unequalled fire and rapture."]

Fire is Pope's element: Pope returns to "the *fire* of the poem" later in the same preface; this is what he says of Chapman: "that which is to be allowed him, and which very much contributed to cover his defects, is a daring fiery spirit that animates his translation, which is something like what we might imagine Homer himself would have writ before he arrived to years of discretion." Of course Pope believed that he himself possessed a daring fiery spirit; and, that being so, his ideal of verse ought not to be an ideal of glaze and polish, "fix'd as in a frost"; his ideal of verse is not very different from Dryden's. Is his practice different? It is not exactly the same, certainly. . . . Did Pope himself in his own practice spoil the old heroic couplet and make it too complete, too separate, too epigrammatic? We may answer this by saying that Pope had many different aims and varieties of style. He certainly knew how to work in mosaic, and Swift describes him so engaged:

Each atom by another struck
All shapes and motions tries,
Till in a lump together stuck
Behold a poem rise.

Sometimes it pleased him to put together independent couplets and make a string of pointed sentences out of them; but nevertheless his fiery spirit would not allow great arguments to be broken up into separate verses and couplets; and in fact he carries on long periods with nearly the same success as Dryden—does not that come out in Belinda's game?—is not that a well-sustained heroic battle? While on the other hand Dryden's strength and eloquence carry with them the same talent for epigram as Pope's. Dryden's brilliance in this respect is not denied by any one; what is less generally recognized is Pope's power of keeping up an argument or a story so that it grows in effect and overrides the single couplets. Neither Dryden nor Pope has always the same wave length; both of them are sometimes choppy, and in both of them you often find the short waves carried on the back of a long swell.

Pope in his *Iliad* took some trouble to escape monotony. He has calendared his experiments in the *Poetical Index* under the head "Versification expressing in the sound the thing describ'd." The interest of this Index and those passages is of course that they show how seriously Pope believed in his own teaching about the sound and the sense, in the *Essay on Criticism*. They also show how he could break the traditional rules of the couplet in order to carry on his story. The regular couplet had been no sooner fixed than it was challenged. Prior in his *Solomon* claimed the freedom of running on the sense: Pope says nothing about this, as Prior does, in his preface, but his verse can be remarkably unlike the ordinary fashion. Here is a quotation from the twenty-third Book of the *Iliad*—a passage which is noted in the Index for three imitations: "the rattling and jumping of carts over a rough and rocky way," "a sudden fall," and "the rattling and crashing of trees falling."

Thus while he spoke, each Eye grew big with Tears:
And now the rosy-finger'd Morn appears,

Shews every mournful Face with Tears o'er-
spread,
And glares on the pale Visage of the Dead.
But *Agamemnon*, as the Rites demand,
With Mules and Waggons sends a chosen Band;
To load the Timber and the Pile to rear,
A Charge consign'd to Merion's faithful Care.
With proper Instruments they take the Road,
Axes to cut, and Ropes to sling the Load.
First march the heavy Mules, securely slow,
O'er Hills, o'er Dales, o'er Crags, o'er Rocks,
they go:
Jumping high o'er the Shrubs of the rough
Ground,
Rattle the clatt'ring bars, and the shockt Axles
bound.
But when arriv'd at *Ida's* spreading Woods,
(Fair *Ida*, water'd with descending Floods)
Loud sounds the Axe, rebounding Strokes on
Strokes;
On all sides round the Forest hurles her Oaks
Headlong. Deep-echoing groan the Thickets
brown;
Then rustling, crackling, crashing, thunder
down.
The Wood the *Grecians* cleave, prepar'd to
burn;
And the slow Mules the same rough Road re-
turn.

Now we see the meaning of that couplet
quoted by Spence from Pope's martyred
epic of *Alcander:*

Shields, helms, and swords all jangle as they
hang
And sound formidinous with angry clang. . . .

Coleridge speaks of Pope's Homer as the
chief source of the conventional pseudo-
poetic diction which drew Wordsworth's
attack. Coleridge, the inventor of "panti-
socracy" and "esemplastic," author of
"defecates to a pure transparency," is not
unfair to Pope's original work; on the contrary he recognizes and praises the excellence and ease of his style when he is
writing for himself. He is probably unjust
to Pope's Homer. Sir Walter Raleigh
makes Milton the chief model of pseudo-
poetic diction: and Pope would not dis-
agree with this; in his postscript to the
Odyssey he speaks of the imitators of Mil-

ton and how they overdo their archaism.
This essay of Pope's is worth reading if
only as an answer to Wordsworth and
Coleridge: it says clearly what Wordsworth was always more or less meaning to
say in his argument about the language of
poetry. Pope himself thought well of this
essay; better, he said, than the preface to
the *Iliad*, where he was too much on the
high horse. It gives a true reading of the
Odyssey as including everything in human
life; it gives a fine description of the poet's
style and language as they change with the
mood and matter of the story and the dialogue. The *Odyssey* is not for him a stiff
formal classical composition: it is as various as Shakespeare. [Quotes parts of six-
teenth and seventeenth, and all of twenty-
third, twenty-fourth, and twenty-sixth paragraphs of Postscript.]

Now what are Pope's original poems
worth, if they are not this same variety?
"The narrow sound of Satire," if I may
use a phrase and figure of Swinburne's,
opens out to a large sea; the beauty of his
satiric poetry is its reflection of the whole
world, not steadily or as the great masters
render it in Epic or Tragedy, but with all
the lights of the greater modes represented
here and there—so that anywhere you may
be caught away, for a moment, to different
regions.

The postscript to the *Odyssey* explains
Pope's ideal of poetic expression, and this
is what he actually obtains in his own
poetry.

He is a master of point and epigram;
but this is not what makes his success.
. . . It would be easy enough to quote
single couplets that are not "distained" by
any jewel of Pope's; and Pope's superiority is not merely in his larger store of
such things. The beauty of Pope's verse is
its living variety; the wave changes its
colour, you might say, as the sun or the
cloud takes it, as it runs green over the
sands, or blue over the deep water. You
never can be certain from the subject what
the language and the tune will be like; and

the advantage of Satire, which is not the highest order of Poetry, is that it can at any moment take the reflection of epic or tragedy. The *Dunciad,* a mock heroic poem more villainous than any of the old ribald travesties of Homer or Virgil, ends in the way we know, beyond all praise

Lo! thy dread empire CHAOS is restor'd:
Light dies before thy uncreating word:
Thy hand, great Anarch, lets the curtain fall—

while before you come to this magnificence you find the couplet which Pope thought the most musical of all his verse:

Lo! where Maeotis sleeps, and hardly flows
The freezing Tanais through a waste of snows.

It does not need the grand style to bring out the strength of Pope; it is shown in a touch here and there, in the effect of a seemingly light and ordinary phrase:

Like Journals, Odes, *and such forgotten things*
As Eusden, Philips, Settle writ of Kings.

The phrase comes again in *Sordello:*

To clear away with such forgotten things
As are an eyesore to the morn,

and it may be through Browning's repetition that we notice it more readily in Pope.

The old device of *Alcander,* the "angry clang," reappears in the description of Blackmore:

What! like Sir Richard, rumbling, rough and fierce,
With ARMS and GEORGE and BRUNSWICK crowd the verse;
Rend with tremendous sound your ears asunder
With Gun, Drum, Trumpet, Blunderbuss and Thunder;
Or nobly wild, with Budgel's fire and force,
Paint Angels trembling round his falling horse.

A different sort of phrasing in the *Essay on Man,* Epistle IV, at the beginning. Before I read it may I say that I think the *Essay on Man* is too much neglected: taken as a curiosity, part of the history of English thought in the eighteenth century, an

example of popular philosophy "in the best of all possible worlds." Some of it is difficult, the sentences, like the reasoning, clogged; some of it is too merely rhetorical:

The lamb thy riot dooms to bleed to-day;

some of it is sinking in poetry:

Why has not man a microscopic eye?
For this plain reason, man is not a fly—

Though this slip is pretty well recovered in what follows. But the Essay contains some of the best of Pope's poetry; the passage on Fame, and this, in a different way:

Oh Happiness! our being's end and aim!
Good, Pleasure, Ease, Content, whate'er thy name,
That something still which prompts the eternal sigh
For which we bear to live, or dare to die,
Which still so near us, yet beyond us lies,
O'erlook'd, seen double, by the fool, and wise.
Plant of celestial seed! if dropt below
Say in what mortal soil thou deign'st to grow:
Fair op'ning to some Court's propitious shine,
Or deep with di'monds in the flaming mine?
Twin'd with the wreaths Parnassian laurels yield
Or reap'd in iron harvests of the field?
Where grows? where grows it not?

Something of Pope's style may be learned from a reference to "iron harvest" as he had used the phrase in his Statius:

How with the serpent's teeth he sow'd the soil,
And reap'd an iron harvest of his toil.

Here it is no more than a conceit; the import, the value, is different in the *Essay on Man.*

I will not quote the passage about his friends in the *Epistle to Arbuthnot,* but I will ask you to remember what Charles Lamb thought of it, and how he read it at that evening party a hundred years ago which is described by Hazlitt in the essay *Of Persons we would wish to have seen.* . . . I must repeat the opening of the *Epistle to Arbuthnot,* for it has long appeared to me, if not the best of Pope at any rate the most expressive of all his confessions. [Quotes 11. 1–26.]

Nothing of Pope's poetry and not the whole of it all together represents fully what he thought and admired. Spenser was one of his favourite poets, all his life long; his praise of Shakespeare goes far beyond the limits of his own poetry. . . .

Pope's poetical work is not the whole of his life. Nor is it, as we are often inclined to think, the dominant force in the poetry of his own time. It is one among many, and his success does not establish a ruling tradition, except for the mechanic warblers. Already in the time of Dryden there were signs of novelty coming on: Atterbury (or the author of the Life of Waller, 1690) recommends blank verse—and Thomson takes the advice. Young competes with Pope in Satire and leaves this for an original policy of his own in the *Night Thoughts*. Prior commanded lyrical forms of Satire unfamiliar to Pope.

> Now let us look for Louis' feather,
> That used to shine so like a star:
> The generals could not get together,
> Wanting that influence great in war.
> O Poet! thou hadst been discreeter,

> Hanging the Monarch's hat so high,
> If thou had'st dubb'd thy star a meteor,
> That did but blaze, and rove, and die!

Gay's address to Pope on the completion of the *Iliad*—"Mr. Pope's welcome from Greece"—is a fresh invention, in the light octaves of Italian burlesque poetry, such as had never been tried in English before, such as the English of Gay's time left unrepeated, to be taken up long after by Frere and Byron:

> Cheer up, my friend, thy dangers now are o'er;
>   Methinks—nay sure, the rising coasts appear;
> Hark, how the guns salute from either shore,
>   As thy trim vessel cuts the Thames so fair:
> Shouts answering shouts from Kent and Essex roar,
>   And bells break loud from ev'ry gust of air:
> Bonfires do blaze, and bones and cleavers ring,
> As at the coming of some mighty king.

It is no depreciation of Pope to recognize that there were other fashions of poetry available in his day. On the contrary, it was a superstitious and exclusive admiration and following of Pope that so long prevented and to this day prevents a right understanding of his varieties of mood and phrase. Dr. Johnson knew better.

T. S. Eliot

Dryden, Pope, and the Material of Poetry [1]

. . . OUR taste in English poetry has been largely founded upon a partial perception of the value of Shakespeare and Milton, a perception which dwells upon sublimity of theme and action. Shakespeare had a great deal more; he had nearly everything to satisfy our various desires for poetry. The point is that the depreciation or neglect of Dryden is not due to the fact that his work is not poetry, but to a prejudice that the material, the feelings, out of which he built is not poetic. Thus Matthew Arnold observes, in mentioning Dryden and Pope together, that "their poetry is conceived and composed in their wits, genuine poetry is conceived in the soul." Arnold was, perhaps, not altogether the detached critic when he wrote this line; he may have been stirred to a defence of his own poetry, conceived and composed in the soul of a mid-century Oxford graduate. Pater remarks that Dryden:

"Loved to emphasize the distinction between poetry and prose, the protest against their confusion coming with somewhat diminished effect from one whose poetry was so prosaic."

But Dryden was right, and the sentence of Pater is cheap journalism. Hazlitt, who had perhaps the most uninteresting mind of all our distinguished critics, says:

"Dryden and Pope are the great masters of the artificial style of poetry in our language, as the poets of whom I have already treated—Chaucer, Spenser, Shakespeare, and Milton—were of the natural."

In one sentence Hazlitt has committed at least four crimes against taste. It is bad enough to lump Chaucer, Spenser, Shakespeare, and Milton together under the denomination of "natural"; it is bad to commit Shakespeare to one style only; it is bad to join Dryden and Pope together; but the last absurdity is the contrast of Milton, our greatest master of the *artificial* style, with Dryden, whose *style* (vocabulary, syntax, and order of thought) is in a high degree natural. And what all these objections come to, we repeat, is repugnance for the material out of which Dryden's poetry is built.

Pope Is Poetry [2]

WHAT "poetry lovers" do not recognize is that their limitation of poetry to the "poetical" is a modern restriction of the romantic age: the romantic age has decided that a great deal of prose is poetry (though I dare say that Burton, and Browne, and De Quincey, and other idols of the poetry-prose romanticists presumed

[1] From "John Dryden" (1922), in *Selected Essays, 1917–1932* by T. S. Eliot, pp. 268–269, copyright, 1932, by Harcourt, Brace and Company, Inc., and reprinted with their permission. (Editor's title.)

[2] From "Introduction: 1928" to *Selected Poems* by Ezra Pound (first published 1928), London, Faber and Faber, 1948, pp. 16, 18. Reprinted by permission of the publisher. (Editor's title.)

that they were writing prose); and conversely that a good deal of poetry is prose. (To me, Pope is poetry and Jeremy Taylor is prose.) . . .

I have met but very few people in my life who really care for poetry; and those few, when they have the knowledge (for they are sometimes quite illiterate people), know how to take from every poet what he has to give, and reject only those poets who whatever they give always pretend to give *more* than they do give; these discerning people appreciate the work of Pope and Dryden (indeed it might be said in our time that the man who cannot enjoy Pope as poetry probably understands no poetry: incidentally, I remember that Pound once induced me to destroy what I thought an excellent set of couplets; for, said he, "Pope has done this so well that you cannot do it better; and if you mean this as a burlesque, you had better suppress it, for you cannot parody Pope unless you can write better verse than Pope—and you can't"). . . .

William Empson

Ambiguity in Pope

AN AMBIGUITY, in ordinary speech, means something very pronounced, and as a rule witty or deceitful. I propose to use the word in an extended sense, and shall think relevant to my subject any verbal nuance, however slight, which gives room for alternative reactions to the same piece of language. . . .

An example of the second type of ambiguity, in word or syntax, occurs when two or more meanings are resolved into one. . . .

I shall now . . . pursue my thesis into the very sanctuary of rationality. During the eighteenth century English poets were trying to be honest, straightforward, sensible, grammatical and plain; thus it is now my business to outwit these poor wretches, and to applaud them for qualities in their writings which they would have been horrified to discover. It is not surprising that this should be possible; "what oft was thought" has a merely delusive simplicity, and "what were ne'er so well expressed" as in a compact antithesis are these shifts and blurred aggregates of thought by which men come to a practical decision. Sometimes they would have called what I call an ambiguity a grace, sometimes a generalisation. How far their ambiguities are typical of their age and method, how fundamental for understanding their verse, it would be more difficult to decide. . . .

It is odd to consider that what is a double meaning in one language is often only a compactness of phrasing in another; that in the sophisticated tongues of many savage tribes you cannot say: "Bring me my gun, the dogs, and three beaters"—using the same verb, and the same inflexion of it, for three such different actions—without being laughed at as a man who has made a bad pun. It is the part of a civilised language to be simplified in structure and generalised in its notions; of a civilised people to keep their linguistic rules and know what they are about; but this must not blind us to the nature of such phrases as

> There thou, great Anna, whom three realms
>   obey,
> Dost sometimes council take, and sometimes tea.
>   (Pope, *Rape of the Lock.*)

where the effect of limited comprehensiveness, of a unity in variety mirrored from the real world, is obtained by putting together two of the innumerable meanings of the word *take*.

> To rest, the cushion and soft dean invite,
> Who never mentions hell to ears polite,
>   (Pope, *Moral Essays*, iv.)

depends on an even slighter, but still genuine enough, ambiguity of the verb.

This way of suggesting grasp of mind, ingenuity, and control over things, this use of a word with several extended meanings so as to contract several sentences into one, is the fundamental device of the Augustan style. The word is usually a verb precisely because the process is conceived as an activity, as a work of the digesting and controlling mind. The *Decline and Fall of the Roman Empire*, for instance, is

From *Seven Types of Ambiguity* (first published 1930), 2nd ed. (revised), New Directions Books, 1947, pp. 1, 48, 68, 70–74, 102, 108–109, 111–112, 117–118, 125–128, 133, 149–151, 241, 256. Reprinted by permission of New Directions; all rights reserved. (Editor's title.)

one enormous panorama of these little witticisms.

Of course, the zeugma is not an eighteenth-century invention, but it was not handled before then with such neatness and consciousness, and had not the same air of being the normal process of thought.

> As such a starre, the *Magi* led to view
> The manger cradled infant, God below;
> By vertue's beams by fame derived from you
> May apt soules, and the worst may, vertue know.

The first *may* means "may be expected to," the second "can if they choose." This is the sort of construction Pope would have handled well; Donne does it very clumsily. Notice, however, that the second *by* may either be parallel to the first, so that the *beams of virtue* are its *fame*, or may be subordinate to it so as to show how the *beams of virtue* came to be distributed. This, and the two uses of *vertue*, corresponding to the two conceptions of it as an attribute of, or personified in, the Countess of Huntingdon, give some weight of thought to an otherwise clumsy construction.

> Your (or you) vertue two vast uses serves,
> It ransomes one sex, and one Court preserves.

"Your virtue serves two uses"; or "you, being virtue itself, serve two uses"; or "you serve (the cause of) virtue two uses." Donne's unfortunate address to the Countess of Bedford may serve to remind us that the eighteenth-century ambiguity was essentially easy and colloquial; it was concerned to exploit, as from a rational and sensible mental state, the normal resources of the spoken language.

Its possible grace and slightness may be shown by a fine detail from the *Rape of the Lock.* When Belinda wins at cards

> The nymph, exulting, fills with shouts the sky;
> The walks, the woods, and long canals reply.
> Oh thoughtless mortals, ever blind to fate,
> Too soon dejected, and too soon elate,

> Sudden these honours shall be snatched away,
> And cursed for ever this victorious day.

Reply may be transitive or intransitive. It is the poet who makes these classical reflections, but, as far as the grammar is concerned, the speaker may as well be the environs of Hampton Court, accustomed as they are to the fall of favourites and the brevity of human glory.

Such a use of the verb may be insisted upon by prepositions or adverbs placed where the different meanings are wanted; this needs no illustration, and my example is intended chiefly to show in how small a compass these typical devices may be employed.

> Oh, if to dance all night, and dress all day,
> Charmed the small pox, or chased old age away,
> Who would not scorn what housewives cares produce,
> Or who would learn one earthly thing of use?
>   (*Rape of the Lock.*)

Here *charmed* at first means "fascinated," so as to make it sit still and do no harm, as one would do to snakes or one's husband; and then, because *chased* insists on the activity of this process, and because *away* is in a prominent position at the end of the line, *charmed* takes on a new meaning as *charmed away*, "removed entirely even when it had already arrived," no doubt by some apparently unreasonable incantation, as one does warts. It is these slight variations of suggestion, I think, that give vivacity to the line.

In the same way, the lyrical outburst of good sense that follows on from this plays continually on the border-line between the first and second types of ambiguity.

> But, since, alas, frail beauty must decay,

This insists it is reasonable by being a tautology: "in so far as beauty is frail it is exposed to decay"; but *frail* from its setting also carries a suggestion of moral as well as physical fragility, which continues to haunt the verses.

Curled, or uncurled, since locks will turn to
grey.

Locks may have been *curled* by art (or
uncurled for that matter), or have been,
to start with, (naturally) *curled;* so that
we have now three ways of dividing up
women—chaste-susceptible, from the first
line; beautiful-ugly, if *uncurled* hair is
out of fashion, and artificial-natural, from
the second. *Will turn to grey* is in part a
simple and inexorable future tense, the
statement of Nature or the poet, and in
part the metre makes it a statement of the
lady; "It *will* turn to grey, the nasty stuff,
I *can't* stop it."

Since, painted, or not painted, all shall fade,

Artificial-natural, with its associate sus-
ceptible-chaste, is now strengthened against
beautiful-ugly as the distinction in question, but not left in possession of the field;
painted might be applied to "meads" in
Pope's dialect, and had not quite lost the
sense of "coloured from whatever cause."

The verb is now only future, as the place
of the ambiguous *will* at the place of emphasis has been taken by *all*. Both these
changes help the crescendo.

And she who scorns a man must die a maid.

The wave as it breaks returns to tautology,
from which the original beautiful-ugly criterion seems to have faded out. It may
combine artificial-natural with wanton-
chaste; "modesty and virtue are no security, because if you don't make the most
of yourself you won't get a husband"; or
may oppose them to one another; "artifi-
ciality and virtue are no security, because
if you think yourself too fine for any of
the available men you won't get a husband
either." The tautology chiefly breaks down
in its tenses, and thus implies that "you
may not want a husband now, whether
because you are too humble or too fanciful, too chaste or too gay, but in the end,
every woman must admit it was what she
needed." In this roundabout way, by not

defining the relation between two criteria
and leaving a loophole in a tautology,
Pope arrives, as did Chaucer in flat sentences, at what may indeed be the fundamental commonplace of poetry, a statement of the limitations of the human situation. "Seeing then the inherent crudity of
all possible earthly happiness, considering
the humility of those demands which can
alone hope to be satisfied . . ."

What then remains, but well our power to use,
And keep good humour still, whate'er we lose?

Well may mean "thoroughly" or "with
moderation," and thus implies a sort of
humility and *good humour* in deciding
which of them is best in any particular
situation. *Still* may mean that we must always keep our balance, always be prepared
to laugh at the absurdity of the world and
our own nature, or *keep* it *still* may mean
that we must be careful not to laugh too
publicly, to give ourselves away by not insisting on our dignity or our rights.[1] Re-
viewing, finally, the three sets of opposites,
we may *lose* beauty, refinement, or virgin-
ity, the lover we had desired, the privacy
we had built up, or the husband it would
have been wise to obtain. . . .

An ambiguity of the third type, considered as a verbal matter, occurs when two
ideas, which are connected only by being
both relevant in the context, can be given
in one word simultaneously. . . .

Where Bentley late tempestuous wont to sport
In troubled waters, but now sleeps in port.
                              (Pope, *Dunciad*, iv.)

The pun is sustained into an allegory by
the rest of the couplet; *tempestuous* and
sport are satirical in much the same way as
the last word. But here, I grant, we have a
simply funny pun; its parts are united by

[1] The idea that the rival idiom "keep still" pokes
up, I now think, was a folly on my part. It would
suggest "Keep good humour from acting," and
Pope would not intend to contradict himself flatly
in a moral sentiment. But *still* ("even then")
does, I think, enrich itself a little with the idea
"calm."

derivation indeed, but too accidentally to give dignity; it jumps out of its setting, yapping, and bites the Master in the ankles.

The eighteenth-century use of a pun is always worldly; to join together so smartly a business and a philosophical notion, a nautical and a gastronomical notion, with an air of having them in watertight compartments in your own mind (each such subject has its rules which save a man from making himself ridiculous, and you have learnt them), so that it seems to you very odd and agile to have jumped from one to the other—all this belongs to the light-weight tattling figure (it is odd it should have been Doctor Johnson's), very ready to form a group and laugh at a man in the street, or to "smoke" Sir Roger de Coverley in the theatre; the man quick to catch the tone of his company, who knows the talk of the town. In each case, too, the pun is used as the climax of a comparison between the subject of the poem, something worldly, and a stock poetical subject with which the writer is less intimately acquainted, which excites feelings simpler and more universal. Wit is employed because the poet is faced with a subject which it is difficult to conceive poetically. . . .

An ambiguity of the third type, then, as a matter concerning whole states of mind, occurs when what it said is valid in, refers to, several different topics, several universes of discourse, several modes of judgment or of feeling. One might call this a general ambiguity of the third type; it includes, for instance, the eighteenth-century puns I have just considered. Now, there are two main ways of constructing such an ambiguity. It may make a single statement and imply various situations to which it is relevant; thus I should call it an ambiguity of this type when an allegory is felt to have many levels of interpretation; or it may describe two situations and leave the reader to infer various things which can be said about both of them; thus I should call it an ambiguity of this

type when an ornamental comparison is not merely using one thing to illustrate another, but is interested in two things at once, and is making them illustrate one another mutually. . . .

The following example may serve to show that Mutual Comparison can degrade instead of elevating both parties. It is not an example of Pope's more poetical satire. The mood is simple, and though the mock-heroic scheme as a whole has a rich imaginative background the pleasure intended here seems only that due to the strength and ingenuity of the attack.

> High on a gorgeous seat that far outshone
> Henley's gilt tub, or Fleckno's Irish throne,
> Or that where on her Curlls the Public pours
> All-bounteous, fragrant grains, and golden showers,
> Great Tibbald sat.
>
> (*Dunciad*, ii.)

Various different situations of mean, vain, and trivial absurdity are being concentrated on the hero by comparison. Now, comparison has two uses, one to show that one thing has more or less of some quality than another, the other to show that the two things are comparable in regard to that quality; an ornamental comparison concentrates on the second of these, and it is the second of these that Pope is exploiting. It may be worth quoting the original Milton:

> High on a Throne of Royal State, which far
> Outshon the wealth of *Ormus* and of *Ind*,
> Or where the gorgeous East with richest hand
> Showers on her Kings *Barbaric* Pearl and Gold,
> Satan exalted sat.
>
> (*Paradise Lost*, ii.)

The comparison with Milton puts Theobald on a "bad eminence" to start with, and then makes him petty and ridiculous because the eminence is too great. His *seat* is then said to *outshine*, and be similar to, the pillory in which *Curll* stood, high and lifted up, and glittering with bad eggs. The word *grains* is chosen to match *pearl*, and mean rotten food in general; *golden showers* may mean that people emptied chamber-pots at him from neighbouring windows. But another world of pettiness and vanity is piled on to these two; *curl* may be a pun meaning one's wig, or the great structures worn by ladies, since the *public* is female: and then the other *throne,* than which the hero's was far more squalid, would be the powdering-tub, *showers* would be hair-oil and *grains* powder. Perhaps one is more conscious here of the difference between the two sorts of *Curl* than of the difference between the powdering-tub and the pillory; I might, therefore, have used this example among the puns, and it may help to show the connection between what I have called the special and general varieties of the same type.

The point of the joke here is the contrast between the different sorts of *throne,* or rather between the attitudes to life, the social settings, represented by them. But . . . the meanings of the symbols are in some degree connected together; their difference is included within a single act of . . . satire. . . .

So far I have dealt with the ambiguity of this type which talks about several things at once; there is also the ambiguity which talks about one thing and implies several ways of judging or feeling about it. This tends to be less rational and self-conscious, therefore less strictly fitted to the third type; it is more dramatic and more aware of the complexities of human judgment. Pope continually makes use of it; partly because, though himself a furious partisan (or rather because of it, so as to pretend he is being fair), he externalises his remarks very completely into statements of fact such as must always admit of two judgments; partly because his statements are so compact, and his rhythmic unit so brief, that he has not always room for an unequivocal expression of feeling. The word "equivocal" is a good one here; much of the force of his satire comes from its pretence of equity. He stimulates the reader's judgment by leaving an apparently unresolved duality in his own—"this is the truth about my poor friend, and you may laugh if you will." The now fashionable attitude to the eighteenth century rather tends to obscure this point; it is true the humour of the period is often savage, but that does not show that the judgments with which it is concerned are crude.

Is Pope sneering or justifying, for instance, in one of the best known of these spare but widely buttressed constructions?—

who, high in Drury Lane,
Lulled by soft zephyrs through the broken pane,
Rhymes e'er he wakes, and prints before term ends,
Obliged by hunger, and request of friends.
(*Epistle to Arbuthnot*)

No one can deny that these words ridicule, but: *obliged by hunger:* I am not sure that they titter; it is only after you have been faced with the dignity of human need that you are moved on to see the grandeur of human vanity. Much recent apologetic for Pope has contented itself with saying how clever it was of the little fellow to be so rude; but to suppose this line means merely "the man must have been a fool as well as a bore, since he was hungry," is not merely an injustice to Pope's humanity, it is a failure to understand the tone he adopts towards his readers.

Soft were my numbers, who could take offence
When pure description held the place of sense? . . .
Yet then did Gildon draw his venal quill.
I wished the man a dinner, and sat still.
(*Epistle to Arbuthnot*)

Good, sympathetic Mr. Pope, one is to think; he has a profound knowledge of human nature. The situation in these two examples is the same; the first stresses his contempt, the second his magnanimity; but in neither can one be sure what proportions are intended. A more verbal expression for this doubt is given in the line about the Goddess of Dulness:

> Where, in nice balance, truth with gold she weighs,
> And solid pudding against empty praise.
>
>   (*Dunciad*, 152.)

Neither *truth* nor *gold,* neither *praise* nor *pudding,* are to be despised, and the pairs may be connected in various ways. A poet is *praised* by posterity for attending to what Pope called *truth;* whereas *gold* and *pudding* are to be gained by flattery. *Gold* may be the weights of the balance with which *truth* is *weighed,* so that the poet will tell any lie that he decides will pay; or all four things may be alike and equally desirable, so that, though the author is hungry and sensible, he is also *truthful* and anxious for his reputation; his proportion of *praise* and *pudding* has to be worked out with honest care. This spectacle, in its humble way, is taken to be charming; so that this version is contemptuous but without the bitterness of the first one. For these versions, *praise* is that of good critics, and it is *empty* beside *pudding* in a sense that would sympathise with the poet's hunger, or as an imagined quotation from him so as to bring him into contempt. But it might be empty as unjustified, as being the *praise* of (that is, from or to) the rich patrons who had bought the compliments; *gold* then takes on the suggestion of contempt, never far from it in Pope's mind, and means "shoddy poetical ornament"; *pudding* is paired with *truth,* in the natural order of the antitheses, and means either the cheap food which is all he would be able to buy, or the *solid* reality of his dull but worthy writings. At any rate, the epithets *solid* and *empty* contradict the antithesis "venal" and "genuine"; it is gay and generous of Pope to have so much sympathy with *pudding;* and it is this detachment from either judgment in the matter (the *truth* such men could tell, the *praise* they could win, is nothing for Pope to be excited

about) which makes the act of *weighing* them seem so absurd.

This process of interpretation may evidently be applied to the feelings a reader imposes on the material; there may be an interest due to the contrast between the stock response and the response demanded by the author. I think myself, in the following border-line case, that I am describing the attitude of Pope, but such an analysis would have achieved its object if it described the attitude only of the majority of his readers. It is that description of a great eighteenth-century mansion in which Pope is apparently concerned only to make its grandeur seem vulgar and stupid.

>   his building is a town,
> His pond an ocean, his parterre a down.
> Who but must laugh, the master when he sees,
> A puny insect, shuddering at a breeze.
>
>   .   .   .   .
>
> My lord advances, with majestic mien,
> Smit with the mighty pleasure to be seen.
>
>   .   .   .   .
>
> But hark, the chiming clocks to dinner call;
> A hundred footsteps scrape the marble hall:
>
>   .   .   .   .
>
> Is this a dinner? this a genial room?
> No, 'tis a temple, and a hecatomb.
>
>   (*Moral Essays*, iv.)

All this is great fun; but before concluding that Pope's better judgment really disapproved of the splendour that he evidently envied, one must remember the saying that as Augustus found Rome, so Dryden found English "brick, and left it marble"; that the Augustans minded about architecture and what Augustus did; that a great part of the assurance and solidity of their attitude to life depended on solid contemporary evidences of national glory. When Pope prophesies the destruction of the building his language takes on a grandeur which reflects back and transfigures it:

> Another age shall see the golden ear
> Embrown the slope, and nod on the parterre,

Deep harvest bury all his pride has planned,
And laughing Ceres reassume the land.

These lines seem to me to convey what is called an intuitive intimacy with nature; one is made to see a cornfield as something superb and as old as humanity, and breaking down dykes irresistibly, like the sea. But, of course, it *embrowns* as with further, more universal, *gilding*, and *nods on the parterre* like a duchess; common things are made dignified by a mutual comparison which entirely depends on the dignity of Canons. The glory is a national rather than a personal one; democracy will *bury* the oligarch; but the national glory is now centred in the oligarch; and if the whole people has been made great, it is through the greatness of the Duke of Chandos.

This seems to me rather a curious example of the mutual comparison which elevates both parties; in this case, it is the admiration latent in a sneer which becomes available as a source of energy for these subsidiary uses: and also an example of how the Wordsworthian feeling for nature can be called forth not by an isolated and moping interest in nature on her own account, but by a conception of nature in terms of human politics. I hope, at any rate, you agree with me that the lines convey this sort of sympathy intensely; that there is some sense of the immensity of harvest through a whole country; that the relief with which the cripple for a moment identifies himself with something so strong and generous gives these two couplets an extraordinary scale. . . .

An ambiguity of the fourth type occurs when two or more meanings of a statement do not agree among themselves, but combine to make clear a more complicated state of mind in the author. Evidently this is a vague enough definition which would cover much of the third type, and almost everything in the types which follow; I shall only consider here its difference from the third type.

One is conscious of the most important aspect of a thing, not the most complicated; the subsidiary complexities, once they have been understood, merely leave an impression in the mind that they were to such-and-such an effect and they are within reach if you wish to examine them. I put into the third type cases where one was intended to be mainly conscious of a verbal subtlety; in the fourth type the subtlety may be as great, the pun as distinct, the mixture of modes of judgment as puzzling, but they are not in the main focus of consciousness because the stress of the situation absorbs them, and they are felt to be natural under the circumstances. Of course, different readers apply their consciousness in different ways, and a line which taken alone would be of the third type may become of the fourth type in its setting; but the distinction, I think, is usually clear. . . .

A [faint] example of the sort of ambiguity in question is supplied by one of Pope's great passages about dowagers, which possesses in a high degree the sensuous beauty that is supposed to have been beyond his powers:

As hags hold sabbats, not for joy but spite,
So these their merry miserable night;
So round and round the ghosts of beauty glide,
And haunt the places where their honour died.
   See how the world its veterans rewards.
A youth of frolics, an old age of cards.
Fair to no purpose, artful to no end,
Young without lovers, old without a friend;
A fop her passion, and her prize a sot;
Alive ridiculous, and dead forgot.
               (*Essay on Women, Ep.* II. 245.)

An impression of febrile and uncontrollable hatred is given to the terrible climax of this passage by the flat, indifferent little words, *fop, sot*, which, if they are to fill out the line, to give it weight, as its meaning and position demand, cannot be dropped with the analytical contempt with which they appear on the printed page; must be hurled at a person conceived as in front of you, to whom you know they are intolerable. Never was the couplet more of a rocking-horse if each line is considered separately; but all the inertia of this flatness is needed to give him strength; never was the couplet given more delicacy of modulation than is here imposed by the mere weight and passion of the sense conveyed. What is so compelling about the passage is the combination within it of two sharply distinguished states of mind; the finicking precision with which the subject-matter is handled; the pity, bitterness, and terror with which the subject-matter must be conceived.

In the third type, two such different moods would both be included, laid side by side, made relevant as if by a generalisation; in the fourth type they react with one another to produce something different from either, and here the reaction is an explosion.

I spoke of "sensuous beauty," thinking of the second couplet quoted, to which a more verbal analysis can be applied. The dowagers may *glide round and round* because they are still dancing, or merely, since they are fixed to the card-table in the next couplet, because they go on and on, in rotation, to the same drawing-rooms. In this way they may at once be conceived as still dancing and yet as at an age when, in those days, they would have had to stop. They are first spoken of as *ghosts* of their dead *beauty*, and will then be thought of as still dancing, since such *ghosts* would still be echoing what they had done in life; but in the next line they are *ghosts* of their dead *honour*, *haunting* a *place* only, and that not so much the ballroom as the card-table. (These *places*, however, are practically the same, so there is an independent ambiguity as to whether they lost their *honour* by cheating at the card-table or making assignations in the ballroom.) The result of this is that the two lines cannot run as simply as they claim to do; *ghosts* means something different for each line, and you must in each case translate the

line back into something said about old ladies, or the transitions will not work. But one is accustomed to this process of immediate translation only in verses of flowery and graceful ornament, so that it is a parody of the manner in which a gallant compliment would have been paid to the ladies, and has a ghastly air of being romantic and charming.

I must not deny that the *ghost* of a dead *beauty* might haunt the place where her *honour* had died, as she might haunt the place where anything that interested her had happened. If you read it like this, there is a touch of that form of wit which caps a sentence with the unexpected word; "you might think she was most distressed at losing her beauty; but no, it's her conscience that troubles the old woman, and well it may." However, I find it very difficult to read the lines like this; they stand too completely parallel and apart, and read like one blow after another.

Or you may say from this parallelism that *beauty* and *honour* are treated as necessary corollaries of one another, the two names being used in the two lines only for variety (as if from the old dictionary interest in synonyms); so that *ghosts of beauty* are the same as *ghosts of honour*, and had necessarily to lose their properties in the same place. Beauty and honour, then, are identical, so that we find ourselves, to our justifiable surprise, in Spenser's fairy-story world of sensuous idealism. There is a sort of subterranean resonance in the verses from the clash of this association; with a feverish anger, like the screws of a liner racing above water, Pope finds himself indeed hagridden by these poor creatures; they excite in him feelings irrelevantly powerful, of waste, of unavoidable futility, which no bullying of its object can satisfy. . . .

It is fair to hold the seventeenth century responsible for most of its ambiguities, because its taste seems to have been curiously free from such critical principles as interpose a judgment before the experience of accepting the poetry is completed. On the other hand, it would often be unprofitable to insist on the ambiguities of Pope, because he expected his readers to prune their minds of any early disorder as carefully as he had pruned his own. My eighteenth-century examples, therefore, have to depend on variations of grammar the authors would have thought trivial, puns which they had intended and thought intelligible, and variations of sense which spring from an effective superficiality in their thought. . . .

I should claim, then, that for those who find this book contains novelties, it will make poetry more beautiful, without their ever having to remember the novelties, or endeavour to apply them. It seems a sufficient apology for many niggling pages.

Geoffrey Tillotson

Pope's Sense of Beauty

PROFESSOR SHERBURN's biography helps one to see continuity in Pope's writing. One of the elements in it that has been neglected by critics is his sense of beauty, and the use of it as material for poetry. Pope may be considered to exemplify, especially as a young poet, certain qualities of two other London-born poets, the Milton of the Horton period and the young Keats. Pope's early conception of the poet is as much as Keats's one of enthusiasm. The ideal poet as he frets through the surface of the *Essay on Criticism* is a bold and fiery spirit with some of the qualities which Pope in the preface to his *Iliad* saw in Homer. A poem for Pope is one

> Where Nature moves and rapture warms the mind;

and in "Windsor Forest" there comes the apostrophe:

> Ye sacred Nine! that all my soul possess,
> Whose raptures fire me, and whose visions bless. . . .

And Pope and Keats both did their poetic reading in the same spirit: Pope confesses that he

> Glows while he reads, but trembles while he writes.

The sonnet on Chapman's Homer sprang from a similar glow and, to take one of Pope's two senses, was written with similar trembling. Pope differs from the young Keats by having a much more continuous regard for orderliness. A poem must be bold but regular. The poet must know when to let fly and when to hold the poem tight. This sense of structure is a rare and valuable thing in English poetry. *Endymion* lacked it, fatally by any high standard. And Pope very nearly produced his own *Endymions*. He told Spence that he "had some thoughts of writing a Persian fable," in which he would "have given a full loose to description and imagination. It would have been a very wild thing. . . ." And these thoughts were amplified in a letter to Judith Cowper:

> I have long had an inclination to tell a fairy tale, the more wild and exotic the better; therefore a *vision*, which is confined to no rules of probability, will take in all the variety and luxuriancy of description you will. . . .

There is a strong element of wildness in the "Temple of Fame," but it is restrained, and wisely restrained.

Like Keats and the young Milton, Pope was a country poet before he was a town poet. We have heard too exclusively of his urban preoccupation with morals and satire. His world of aesthetic experience was as extensive as that of any other poet. Pope is held to be deficient in a sense of beauty, in the amount of beauty he experienced and in the quality of that experience. Actually he was as sensitive to aesthetic experience as the young Milton, and probably as sensitive to it as the young Keats. Spence preserved some important fragments of his aesthetics. He shows Pope on the Thames receiving "That Idea of the Picturesque, from the swan just gilded with the sun amidst the shade of a tree over the

Reprinted by permission from *Essays in Criticism and Research*, Cambridge University Press, 1942, pp. 88–98, with a few verbal changes by the author; first printed in *The* [London] *Times Literary Supplement* in 1934. (Editor's title.)

water." And another remark, almost Wordsworthian in imputing to education the spoiling of the natural instincts:

A tree is a nobler object than a prince in his coronation robes. . . . Education leads us from the admiration of beauty in natural objects, to the admiration of artificial (or customary) excellence. . . . I don't doubt but that a thoroughbred lady might admire the stars, *because* they twinkle like so many candles at a birth-night.

Pope is seen in Professor Sherburn's second chapter (1705–1715) to be as completely environed with lane, wood and field as Milton was in the vacations and after leaving Cambridge, and as Keats liked to be. Gay in 1713 inscribed his "Rural Sports" to Pope: to

You, who the sweets of rural life have known, [And] despise th' ungrateful hurry of the town. . . .

In the "Pastorals" and "Windsor Forest," Pope is as warmly in love with natural sights and sounds as any of those pastoralists and country-drawn poets who are always breaking into seventeenth-century poetry with their sunny landscapes. Pope asks for:

　　　　　. . . sequester'd scenes,
The bow'ry mazes, and surrounding greens:
. . . Thames's banks, which fragrant breezes fill,
Or where ye Muses sport on Cooper's Hill. . . .
I seem thro' consecrated walks to rove,
I hear soft music die along the grove.
Led by the sound, I roam from shade to shade,
By god-like Poets venerable made. . . .

Pope made the most of the usual training for a poet, things of acknowledged beauty to see, things of acknowledged beauty to read.

The thoroughbred lady might like stars because of candles. Pope preferred stars, but had his aesthetic use for candlelight. He carried his sense of beauty further than any previous poet by taking it indoors with him and employing it on anything made by the inspired hand of man. This was one of the easy means of transition to "town" poetry. In the work of utilitarian silversmith or carver Pope took a delight that is new and valuable for English poetry. George Herbert, Herrick and Waller had touched part of this new area for poetry, but Pope is the first poet who shows himself worthy of looking at the work of the anonymous Inigo Joneses and Grinling Gibbonses of the silver workshops. Pope provides a logical extension of one aspect of renaissance humanism. The Elizabethans were fond of describing their dolphin chambers. Pope sees the things on a sophisticated table to be lovely, man's hand being god-like even in the commonplace:

For lo! the board with cups and spoons is crown'd,
The berries crackle, and the mill turns round.
On shining altars of Japan they raise
The silver lamp; the fiery spirits blaze.
From silver spouts the grateful liquors glide,
While China's earth receives the smoking tide. . . .

It is part of the way that everything for Pope is centralized in man, in men, in human character and the visible instruments upon which human character orchestrates its fine or broken music. Pope is often laughing at man-made beauty since it is so often misused by man, since it so often exemplifies the proud canker in his soul. But in itself he finds it beautiful.

This experience of indoor beauty—or of beauty contrived by man out of doors, in gardens, for instance—was included no doubt under "plains" in Wordsworth's famous remark about Pope's neglecting the heights—Wordsworth allowed that the heights were within Pope's reach. But it is what one sees in the plains that matters, as it is equally what one sees in the heights. One might as well quarrel with Manet for wasting time with the bar of the Folies Bergère when there were mountains sawing the skies, as quarrel with Pope for the Hampton Court interior.

Besides this extension of beauty on one of its boundaries, Pope may claim to be a "nature poet" in a way disconcerting to the romantic nature-poets. In the same way that Swift saw more in animals than any previous writer except the author of *King Lear,* so Pope saw more in insects than any other poet except perhaps Gray. Insects are everywhere in Pope's poetry. Swift sees men often as beasts, as rats or wolves or yahoos. Pope sees men often as insects, and there is no doubt about the natural liveliness of his vision:

Satire or sense alas! can *Sporus* feel?
Who breaks a butterfly upon a wheel?

and the answer that neglects the implied denial:

Yet let me flap this bug with gilded wings,
This painted child of dirt that stinks and
  stings . . .
[Who] at the ear of Eve, familiar Toad,
Half froth, half venom, spits himself
  abroad. . . .

Man is "a puny insect shivering at a breeze," "an industrious bug,"

And lo the wretch! whose vile, whose insect lust
Laid this gay daughter of the Spring in dust.

The first motto chosen for the *Dunciad* was the famous stanza of the *Faerie Queene,* in which the shepherd "mars" the play of gnats, a stanza Pope recollected in the "Epilogue to the Satires":

Ye tinsel Insects! whom a Court maintains,
That counts your Beauties only by your Stains,
Spin all your Cobwebs o'er the Eye of Day!
The Muse's wing shall brush you all away. . . .

One might take these instances to show to what use Pope put his perception, whether of beautiful or unpleasant things. Pope is seldom exclusively interested in beauty, and in his greatest poetry he is seldom interested in beauty for its own sake. (This is also true of his strong interest in the beauty of versification.) To speak more precisely, Pope's interest in beauty is only

allowed to be total on momentary occasions. If his poem has brought him to a point where he can write with his eye full on beautiful things and forget all else, he takes the chance to be as purely a poet of beauty as ever Keats was. His excursion into pure beauty may be limited by its place in the poem. It is tied, so to speak, at both ends. But inside that prescribed space, or rather time—perhaps the five seconds of a couplet—the chance for the perfect realization of beauty is infinite. The astonishing thing is that in these flashes Pope can cover such large areas. In the early poems he gives himself, as he saw later, too many chances. He came to see, as Keats came to see, that "pure description" should not hold "the place of sense." But the descriptions that he did write are fine and varied. The pheasant in "Windsor Forest" is as brilliantly done as Chaucer's chanticleer. Then there is the throne of Fame, and this northern simile raised on a basis of his reading in books of travel:

So Zembla's rocks (the beauteous work of
  frost)
Rise white in air, and glitter o'er the coast;
Pale suns, unfelt, at distance roll away,
And on th' impassive ice the light'nings play:
Eternal snows the growing mass supply,
Till the bright mountains prop th' incumbent
  sky;
As Atlas fix'd, each hoary pile appears,
The gather'd winter of a thousand years.

It is noteworthy that when Nova Zembla is mentioned in the later poems it is by name only. In those later poems the element of beauty is restricted. The point here is that that element is as intensely perceived as in the works of any great poet. Because it is all controlled, critics have been apt to think there was nothing to control.

Pope controls the element of beauty not only in its amount but in its manner of expression. He formularizes the expression of it to fit the geometrical subtleties of his couplets. And, moreover, he often itemizes it as part of a process analogous to deduction. He begins with a general idea and applies it to the external world, selecting by a process of itemization. This is really Ovid's way in the *Metamorphoses*. Daphne, Mirrha or Dryope become trees, and the process is followed item by item. This is part of Dryden's translation of the tenth book:

> For while she spoke, the Ground began to rise,
> And gather'd round her Feet, her Leggs, and Thighs:
> Her Toes in Roots descend, and spreading wide,
> A firm Foundation for the Trunk provide:
> Her solid Bones convert to solid Wood,
> To pith her Marrow, and to Sap her Blood:
> Her Arms to Boughs, her Fingers change their Kind,
> Her tender Skin is harden'd into Rind.

This becomes the method of much of Pope's description—Sandys's Ovid was a favourite book of his childhood, Dryden had translated several of Ovid's stories, and Pope himself did early translations from Ovid. Here are some of his itemized descriptions:

> Oft in her glass [i.e. a stream's] the musing shepherd spies
> The headlong mountains and the downward skies,
> The wat'ry landscape of the pendant woods,
> And absent trees that tremble in the floods;
> In the clear azure gleam the flocks are seen,
> And floating forests paint the waves with green,
> Thro' the fair scene roll slow the lingering streams,
> Then foaming pour along, and rush into the Thames.

Later it is the manner of the "Eloisa" setting:

> But o'er the twilight groves, and dusky caves,
> Long-sounding aisles, and intermingled graves,
> Black Melancholy sits, and round her throws
> A death-like silence, and a dread repose:
> Her gloomy presence saddens all the scene,
> Shades ev'ry flow'r, and darkens ev'ry green,
> Deepens the murmur of the falling floods,
> And breathes a browner horror on the woods.

Later still it is the manner of the *Moral Essays:*

> Grove nods at grove, each Alley has a brother,
> And half the platform just reflects the other.
> The suff'ring eye inverted Nature sees,
> Trees cut to Statues, Statues thick as trees;
> With here a Fountain, never to be play'd;
> And there a Summer-house, that knows no shade;
> Here Amphitrite sails thro' myrtle bow'rs;
> There Gladiators fight, or die in flow'rs;
> Un-water'd see the drooping sea-horse mourn,
> And swallows roost in Nilus' dusty Urn.

Pope's sense of beauty is almost always incorporated into his sense of interest. He sees meaning among things. This is one of the several seventeenth-century elements in his poetry, and its presence forbids him to discard entirely the methods of the metaphysical poets. Not that his meaning is of the same kind as that of Donne or Herbert. It is his process which is often theirs. The sensuous world is as important to him as it is to them because it coordinates itself with the strength of his meaning. This is often the explanation of his similes. They are seldom decorations for their own sake, even when they are parodies of epic similes. They are usually sudden and surprising intricacies of the external world that an intricate thought has magnetized to itself. They are the same in kind as the fine "homely" similes in the *Biographia Literaria*. The material of these similes may be beautiful or unpleasant, but whether it is one or the other is irrelevant, is accidental. The thought has been sufficiently intense to coalesce with that detail of the external world which is, so to speak, the sole example of its law:

> For wit and judgment often are at strife,
> Tho' meant each other's aid, like man and wife.

Or the law may have two manifestations:

> Or, if to Wit a coxcomb make pretence,
> Guard the sure barrier between that and Sense;
> Or quite unravel all the reas'ning thread,
> And hang some curious cobweb in its stead!

As, forc'd from wind-guns, lead itself can fly,
And pond'rous slugs cut swiftly thro' the sky;
As clocks to weight their nimble motion owe,
The wheels above urg'd by the load below. . . .

Pope uses his acquaintance with beauty or "interest" where it is needed. And so with every other element in his poetry. One of the most subtle things in poetry is the way in which a poem by Pope is multiple in its layers of significance. Pope is usually doing several things at once. He is writing what he wants to say on his theme. This, of course, is what any author is doing; but for Pope the saving of what he had to say entailed the saying of it in an intensive manner that has seldom been completely that of any other poet. Shenstone said that, more than any other writer, Pope had the art of condensing sense, though Dr Johnson, sitting wet through in a hut in Scotland, did not agree with him. Again, Pope was concerning himself with the fine mechanics of his verse. Every poet must be attentive on this point. But Pope was unusually attentive. He distinguished, he told Spence, between a sweetness and softness in versification, which will serve to indicate the gradations of his sensitiveness to sound. Then, usually he was writing in imitation of some poet or poetic form. The *Rape of the Lock* and the *Dunciad* are miniature epic poems, and the detailed tallying is effected by a technical mastery which, being exercised on materials so lively in themselves, recalls Mozart. The speech of Clarissa, added in the 1717 version of the *Rape,* is a close parody of Pope's own earlier translation of the speech of Sarpedon to Glaucus in the *Iliad.* The *Imitations of Horace* show the poet bound hand and foot and yet dancing as if free. These do not exhaust the sum of his activities. He is always eager to adapt the phrases of earlier poets. It was almost a principle with him. As an example of this one might take the line:

[Till] Alma Mater lie dissolv'd in Port.

This expression takes its rise from Ovid. Line 612 of Book xi of the *Metamorphoses,* concluding the description of the cave of Sleep, reads:

Quo cubat ipse Deus, membris languore solutis.

Sandys translates by:

Here lay the lazie God, dissolu'd in rest.

When Dryden came to the same line in his translation he avoided the literal perfection of Sandys, and wrote:

. . . where lay the God
And slept supine, his limbs display'd abroad.

But he remembered the phrase when translating the story of Cymon and Iphigenia from Boccaccio, and at line 550 spoke of

. . . Men dissolv'd in ease.

So far, in Sandys and Dryden, the phrase has remained virtually static. Pope provides it with its culmination. His line requires the cooperation of the reader's memory for all its juices to be at their most piquant. This kind of imitation was as important for Pope's verse as any other element. And finally, added to all these, there was his continuous attempt to control his poem into shapeliness.

Since all these activities are usually found working together in a poem of Pope's this is the best answer for anyone who considers a simple cause like ill-nature to have accounted for his satiric poetry. Pope had his hatreds as his contemporaries had theirs for him. But his sense of the strenuous requirements of his verse promoted the personal grudge into a larger emotional context, the disinfecting context of hard work, and finally of great poetry. When one reads the character of Sporus, one's eyes are not on Hervey. It is as much as they can do to receive the fire of the words. Hervey's character is for Pope an entrance into a brilliantly sensuous world every atom of which is vital, a world as exciting to the aesthetic sense as those of the "Nun's Priest's Tale" or of "Lamia."

Moreover, hatred as an inspiration for Pope's satire has been accorded too much importance. The emotion of pity is often as powerfully at work:

Who would not weep, if Atticus were he?

Or this from "Of the Characters of Women":

Asham'd to own they gave delight before,
Reduc'd to feign it, when they give no more:
As Hags hold Sabbaths, less for joy than spite.
So these their merry, miserable Night;
Still round and round the Ghosts of Beauty
  glide,
And haunt the places where their Honour died.

Satiric poetry such as this affects the primary human emotions, even in Matthew Arnold's sense that limited the meaning to the nobler of these emotions. The terms "moral" and "satiric" poetry have put off readers for too long. One's face, if it responded to this poetry (and the face is apt to respond privately to Pope) would wear a complicated smile, or a look of complicated solemn intensity. Hazlitt, the pro-foundest of all critics on the *Rape,* did not know whether to laugh or to weep over the poem. Pope added a "moral" to it in the 1717 edition:

Oh! if to dance all night, and dress all day,
Charm'd the small-pox, or chas'd old-age away;
Who would not scorn what huswife's cares pro-
  duce,
Or who would learn one earthly thing of use?
To patch, nay ogle, might become a Saint,
Nor could it sure be such a sin to paint.
But since, alas! frail beauty must decay,
Curl'd or uncurl'd, since locks will turn to grey;
Since painted, or not painted, all shall fade,
And she who scorns a man, must die a maid;
What then remains, but well our pow'r to use,
And keep good humour still whate'er we
  lose? . . .

This is indeed (to use a phrase that comes twice in his poetry) "the language of his heart." And that language is habitual with him. No other poet has found his sense of beauty so closely and continuously allied to his sense of human values. No other poet has put or answered the question how to live with tenderer concern and more pointed wisdom. In his trembling eye a virtue was as dear as a flower.

F. R. Leavis

Pope's Poise

POPE has had bad luck. Dryden, fortunate in the timeliness of Mr. Mark Van Doren's book, was enlisted in the argument against the nineteenth century. It was an opportunity; the cause was admirable and *Homage to John Dryden* admirably served it (though Mr. Eliot, who—or so it seems to me—has always tended to do Dryden something more than justice, was incidentally, perhaps accidentally, unfair to Pope). The homage announcing, on the other hand, Pope's rehabilitation was left to Bloomsbury, and Pope, though he has more to offer the modern reader than Dryden and might have been enlisted in the argument with certainly not less effect, was taken over, an obvious property, by the postwar cult of the *dix-huitième*—an opportunity for Lytton Strachey and Miss Sitwell.

Such attention as he has received from critics qualified to appreciate him—an aside from Mr. Middleton Murry,[1] a note by Mr. Edgell Rickword,[2] a paragraph or two of Empsonian analysis [3]—has been casual. It is true that what is offered by these three critics (and there is not a great deal more to record) would, if considered, be enough to establish an intelligent orientation to Pope. And Pope's achievement being so varied, I can hardly pretend to attempt more than this. Keeping in view the

[1] See the essay on Collins in *Countries of the Mind.*

[2] In a review of *The Oxford Book of Eighteenth Century Verse* reprinted in *Towards Standards of Criticism* (edited by the present writer).

[3] *Seven Types of Ambiguity*, pp. 161–2.

purpose of the book and the necessary limits of space, I can aim at little more than to suggest coercively the re-orientation from which a revaluation follows; if more, to indicate something of Pope's range and variety.

"Re-orientation," here, envisages in particular the classification "satirist." It may be no longer necessary to discuss whether satire can be poetry, and we may have entirely disposed of Matthew Arnold; nevertheless, when Pope is classed under "Satire" it is still with a limiting effect, as if he did only one kind of thing, and that involving definite bounds and a restricted interest. So there is point in considering to begin with a poem of an excellence that is obviously not satiric.

The rare fineness of the *Elegy to the Memory of an Unfortunate Lady* has not had the recognition it deserves. It is praised commonly (when praised) for a "pathetic" power distinguishing it from the body of Pope's work, but this does not appear to recommend it even to Miss Sitwell. In fact, though to condemn the manner as declamatory is no longer the thing, there is something about it that is found unengagingly outmoded. I remember to have heard, incredulously, a theory, purporting to come from a critic of high repute, that is worth mentioning because it calls attention to certain essential characteristics of the poem. The theory was that Pope opened in all solemnity, but finding it impossible to continue in so high-flown a strain without smiling at himself (he had, after all, a sense of humour), slipped in a qualifying element

Reprinted by permission from *Revaluation: Tradition & Development in English Poetry*, London, Chatto & Windus, 1936, pp. 68–91. (Editor's title.)

of burlesque and achieved a subtle total effect analogous to that of *Prufrock*. The evidence? Well, for example, this:

As into air the purer spirits flow,
And sep'rate from their kindred dregs below;
So flew the soul to its congenial place,
Nor left one virtue to redeem her Race.

The percipient reader, one gathered, smiled here, and, if it were pointed out that "dregs" turned "the purer spirits" into a ludicrous metaphor, the less percipient would smile also.

Nevertheless, the reader who sees the relevance here of remarking that Pope was born in the seventeenth century will not be inclined to smile any more than at

But ah! my soul with too much stay
Is drunk, and staggers in the way

in Vaughan's *The Retreat*. If it had never occurred to one that the image could strike any reader as funny, it is not because of the lulling effect of Pope's orotund resonances, but because, by the time one comes to the lines in question, one has been so potently reminded of Pope's Metaphysical descent. The preceding lines are actually those quoted by Mr. Middleton Murry as illustrating the Metaphysical element in Pope:

Most souls, 'tis true, but peep out once an age,
Dull sullen pris'ners in the body's cage:
Dim lights of life, that burn a length of years
Useless, unseen, as lamps in sepulchres;
Like Eastern Kings a lazy state they keep,
And close confin'd to their own palace, sleep.

Mr. Murry's observation is just. Pope is as much the last poet of the seventeenth century as the first of the eighteenth. His relationship to the Metaphysical tradition is aptly suggested by his *Satires of Dr. Donne Versified*: bent as he was (with Dryden behind him) on being the first "correct" poet, Metaphysical "wit"—the essential spirit of it—was at the same time congenial to him, more so than to Dryden; and what is suggested in the undertaking

to "versify" Donne he achieved in his best work. In it subtle complexity is reconciled with "correctness," his wit is Metaphysical as well as Augustan, and he can be at once polite and profound.

In the passage first quoted one is not merely solemnly impressed by the striking images; their unexpectedness and variety —the "heterogeneous ideas" that are "yoked together"—involve (on an adequate reading) a play of mind and a flexibility of attitude that make such effects as that of "dregs" acceptable when they come: there is an element of surprise, but not the shock that means rejection (complete or ironically qualified) of the inappropriate. Seriousness for Pope, for the Metaphysicals, for Shakespeare, was not the sustained, simple solemnity it tended to be identified with in the nineteenth century; it might include among its varied and disparate tones the ludicrous, and demand, as essential to the total effect, an accompanying play of the critical intelligence. So in these lines of Pope: the associations of "peep" are not dignified, and one's feelings towards the "souls" vary, with the changing imagery, from pitying contempt for the timorous peepers, through a shared sense (still qualified with critical contempt, for one is not oneself dull and sullen) of the prisoners' hopeless plight, and a solemn contemplation in the sepulchral couplet of life wasted among shrivelled husks, to that contempt mixed with humour and a sense of opulence that is appropriate to the Kings lazing in their palaces.

The Kings are at least dignified, and they make the transition to the complete dignity of the Lady, who enters again in the next couplet:

From these perhaps (ere nature bade her die)
Fate snatch'd her early to the pitying sky.
As into air the purer spirits flow, *etc.*

But her dignity is not a precarious one, to be sedulously guarded from all possibly risible associations. The "mean" element in the texture of the previous passage can be safely carried on in "dregs." The very violence of this, directed as it is upon her contemptible family ("her Race"), draws the attention away from the value it gives, retrospectively, to "spirits," though enough of this value is felt to salt a little, as it were, the sympathetically tender nobility that is opposed to "dregs."

Indeed, the successful reconciliation of so formally exalted a manner with such daring shifts and blends is conditioned by this presence of a qualifying, seasoning element. This presence is wit. We have a clear sense of its being generated (to take the process at its most observable) in the play of thought and image glanced at above, from "Most souls" to "sleep." The changes of tone and attitude imposed on the reader (consider, for instance, that involved in passing from "souls" to "peep" in the first line) result in an alertness; a certain velleity of critical reserve in responding; a readiness for surprise that amounts in the end to an implicit recognition, at any point, in accepting what is given, of other and complementary possibilities. It becomes plain, in the light of such an account, why we should find ourselves describing as "mature" the sensibility exhibited by verse in which wit is an element, and also why, in such verse, a completely serious poetic effect should be able to contain suggestions of the ludicrous such as for Gray, Shelley or Matthew Arnold would have meant disaster.

The use here of the term "wit" has its prompting, of course, in the seventeenth century, when wit was an established mode, cultivated as such by the practitioner of verse. "An established mode"—it is extremely difficult in compressed statement to avoid misleading simplifications: the line running from Ben Jonson was as important as that running from Donne. Yet, as the first chapter of this book will have conveyed, to speak of two is also misleading; what merging there was is suggested well enough by the mention of Carew and

Marvell. "Wit" comprehended not only the audacities of Donne, but also the urbane critical poise of Ben Jonson. A like poise is an essential characteristic of Marvell's best Metaphysical work, and is developed, as it were, for inspection in the *Horatian Ode*, that perfect triumph of civilization, unique in English, beside which the Augustanism of Pope appears to have a note of provinciality (one may at any rate say that in comparison with Pope's, which is strongly "period," Marvell's is timeless).

It is, then, plain enough that Pope's reconciliation of Metaphysical wit with the Polite has antecedents.

> A Soul hung up, as 'twere, in Chains
> Of Nerves, and Arteries, and Veins.
> Tortur'd, besides each other part,
> In a vain Head, and double Heart.

—The familiar turn of that close, a turn not confined to Marvell, of whom, however, the supreme representative of seventeenth-century urbanity, it is most characteristic, surely has affinities with a characteristic effect of Pope's longer couplet:

> First slave to Words, then vassal to a Name,
> Then dupe to party; child and man the same;
> Bounded by Nature, narrow'd still by Art,
> A trifling head, and a contracted heart.[4]

But such particularity of resemblance may hinder as much as help; it may be better to adduce something as insistently unlike anything Pope could have written as King's

> 'Tis true, with shame and grief I yield,
> Thou like the *Vann* first took'st the field
> And gotten hast the victory
> In thus adventuring to dy
> Before me, whose more years might crave
> A just precedence in the grave.

A certain crisp precision of statement, a poised urbanity of movement and tone, that relates this passage to the other two becomes very apparent in the last line. The effect is as of an implicit reference, even here in King where personal feeling is so

4 *The Dunciad*, Bk. IV, 1. 501.

indubitably strong, of the immediate feeling and emotion to a considered scale of values—a kind of critical "placing," as it were.

A kindred effect begins, in the latter half of the first paragraph, to make itself felt even in the rather histrionic exaltation of Pope's opening: [5]

> Is it, in heav'n, a crime to love too well?
> To bear too tender, or too firm a heart,
> To act a Lover's, or a Roman's part?
> Is there no bright reversion in the sky,
> For those who greatly think, or bravely die?

Enough at any rate is there to make possible the marvellously sure transition to the passage, quoted by Mr. Murry and examined above, which constitutes most of the second paragraph.

It is time now to consider the declamatory heightening characteristic of the poem. It compels attention to itself again at about the thirteenth line, leading as it does to those magnificent exaggeration-effects:

> But thou, false guardian of a charge too good,
> Thou, mean deserter of thy brother's blood!
> See on these ruby lips the trembling breath,
> These cheeks now fading at the blast of death:
> Cold is that breast which warm'd the world before,
> And those love-darting eyes must roll no more.
> Thus, if Eternal justice rules the ball,
> Thus shall your wives, and thus your children fall;
> On all the line a sudden vengeance waits,
> And frequent hearses shall besiege your gates.
> There passengers shall stand, and pointing say,
> (While the long fun'rals blacken all the way)
> Lo these were they, whose souls the Furies steel'd,
> And curs'd with hearts unknowing how to yield.

The success of these effects depends, it is clear, upon the heightened tone and man-

ner, or rather it is a matter of complementary manifestations.

No modern poet, of course, could adopt successfully so lofty and formal a decorum, though the modern reader should have no difficulty in living into it. Pope could find it natural because it was sanctioned by contemporary convention. So obvious a statement may seem not worth making, but there are implications that still, apparently, need insisting on. It is not a question of merely literary convention, any more than Pope's "correctness" is to be discussed as Lytton Strachey elegantly affects to discuss it,[6] in prosodic terms (one cannot say "technical"—technique in any serious sense does not exist for discussion at that level), as consummating a bent towards regularity and symmetry—a bent developing out of the recognition that the "possibilities" of blank verse were "exhausted." The development was in English life, and the "correctness" of Pope's literary form derives its strength from a social code and a civilization. With Dryden begins the period of English literature when form is associated with Good Form, and when, strange as it may seem to us, Good Form could be a serious preoccupation for the intelligent because it meant not mere conformity to a code of manners but a cultivated sensitiveness to the finest art and thought of the time.

The Augustans could be so innocently unaware of the conventional quality of the code—it was "Reason" and "Nature"— because they were in complete accord about fundamentals. Politeness was not merely superficial; it was the service of a culture and a civilization, and the substance and solid bases were so undeniably there that there was no need to discuss them or to ask what was meant by "Sense." Augustanism is something narrower, less fine and less subtle, than what Marvell stands for, but it has a corresponding strength of concentration and single-mindedness.

If Pope too, then, could be both elegant

---

[5] The first part of the paragraph runs:
> What beck'ning ghost, along the moon-light shade
> Invites my steps, and points to yonder glade?
> 'Tis she!—but why that bleeding bosom gored,
> Why dimly gleams the visionary sword?
> Oh ever beauteous, ever friendly! tell, *etc.*

[6] See his Leslie Stephen lecture on Pope.

and insolent, the elegance and the insolence were not inane. How firmly he realized the substance, and how habitually present to him were the positive bases, one is apt to find most strikingly evidenced in the neighbourhood of his most spirited satiric passages. For instance, there is the culminating passage, in *Epistle IV (Of the Use of Riches,* to Richard Boyle, Earl of Burlington), of the attack on Canons:

> But hark! the chiming Clocks to Dinner call;
> A hundred footsteps scrape the marble Hall:
> The rich Buffet well-colour'd Serpents grace,
> And gaping Tritons spew to wash your face.
> Is this a dinner? this a Genial room?
> No, 'tis a Temple, and a Hecatomb.
> A solemn Sacrifice, perform'd in state,
> You drink by measure, and to minutes eat.
> So quick retires each flying course, you'd swear
> Sancho's dread Doctor and his Wand were there.
> Between each Act the trembling salvers ring,
> From soup to sweet-wine, and God bless the King.
> In plenty starving, tantaliz'd in state,
> And complaisantly help'd to all I hate,
> Treated, caress'd, and tir'd, I take my leave,
> Sick of his civil Pride from Morn to Eve;
> I curse such lavish cost, and little skill,
> And swear no Day was ever past so ill.

After the sneering, destructive gusto of this one can for a moment hardly credit that the next four lines are unironically solemn, so complete is the change of tone:

> Yet hence the Poor are cloth'd, the Hungry fed;
> Health to himself, and to his Infants bread
> The Lab'rer bears: What his hard Heart denies,
> His charitable Vanity supplies.

If there were any doubt it would be settled at once by what follows. This is a passage that occasions some of the finest criticism in Mr. Empson's *Seven Types of Ambiguity* (pp. 161–2):

> Another age shall see the golden Ear
> Embrown the Slope, and nod on the Parterre,
> Deep Harvests bury all his pride has plann'd,
> And laughing Ceres re-assume the land.

Mr. Empson's subtle commentary, which is immediately relevant and should be looked up, ends with a hope for agreement on the part of the reader that there is conveyed in these lines a feeling for nature, called forth "by a conception of nature in terms of human politics"; "that there is some sense of the immensity of harvest through a whole country; that the relief with which the cripple for a moment identifies himself with something so strong and generous gives these two couplets an extraordinary scale."

The qualification and addition that I would make are that the cripple may be over-stressed and that there is a more general significance. The relevant commentary for my argument is offered implicitly by Pope himself in the lines that come next:

> Who then shall grace, or who improve the Soil?
> Who plants like Bathurst, or who builds like Boyle.
> 'Tis Use alone that sanctifies Expense,
> And Splendour borrows all her rays from Sense.
>   His Father's Acres who enjoys in peace,
> Or makes his Neighbours glad, if he increase:
> Whose cheerful Tenants bless their yearly toil,
> Yet to their Lord owe more than to the soil;
> Whose ample Lawns are not asham'd to feed
> The milky heifer and deserving steed;
> Whose rising Forests, not for pride or show,
> But future Buildings, future Navies, grow:
> Let his plantations stretch from down to down,
> First shade a Country, and then raise a Town.
>   You too proceed! . . .

—And so it goes on, in fourteen more lines of hortatory grandeur, to the end.

Formal compliment in the Grand Style, some one may remark, was in order in such a piece, particularly in the close; it was in the convention of the period. It was. The period was one that could support such a convention, and Pope here (that is the point) has the strength of his period. That the positives so magnificently asserted are asserted more than conventionally we know from the force and life of the passage, which is essentially continuous with those superb prelusive lines appraised in Mr. Empson's analysis. The same inspiration informs the whole: the ideal (generally shared and not hopelessly removed from the actual) of a civilization in which Art and Nature, Beauty and Use, Industry and Decorum, should be reconciled, and humane culture, even in its most refined forms, be kept appropriately aware of its derivation from and dependence on the culture of the soil. The aesthetic, the moral and the utilitarian are characteristically associated in the "milky heifer and deserving steed," which graze the "ample lawns" of an eighteenth-century landscape, itself a work of art.

From the supply-varying, continually surprising, play of satiric ridicule to these resonant and decorous elevations (where "steed" comes naturally) Pope can pass with perfect ease and sureness of transition —a testimony not only to the stable poise that makes the elevations safe, but, reciprocally, to something in the satire.

The commentary called for by the exalted decorum of the *Elegy* is, then, implicitly provided by Pope himself:

'Tis Use alone that sanctifies Expense,
And Splendour borrows all her rays from Sense.[7]

Pope was at one with a society to which these were obvious but important truths. So supported, he could sustain a formal dignity such as, pretended to, would make a modern ridiculous. "Use" represents robust moral certitudes sufficiently endorsed by the way of the world, and "Sense" was a light clear and unquestionable as the sun.

---

[7] Cf. See! sportive fate, to punish awkward pride,
Bids Bubo build, and sends him such a Guide:
A standing sermon, at each year's expense,
That never Coxcomb reach'd Magnificence!
You show us, Rome was glorious, not profuse,
And pompous buildings once were things of Use.

(From the same epistle.)

There is no need to illustrate further the variety of tone from passage to passage in the *Elegy*, or the sureness of the transitions. After various tones of declamation, we pass through the passage anticipating (or furnishing) an eighteenth-century mode, associated with Collins and Gray, of conventional elegiac sentiment to the deeply moving final paragraph, in which the strong personal emotion, so firmly subdued throughout to the "artificial" form and manner, insists more and more on its immediately personal intensity.

It is time now to turn to the satirist. What in the foregoing page or two may have appeared excessively elementary will be recognized, perhaps, in its bearing on the satire, to serve at least some purpose. For, granting Pope to be pre-eminently a satirist and to enjoy as such what favour he does enjoy, one cannot easily find good reasons for believing that an intelligent appreciation of satiric poetry is much commoner to-day than it was among the contemporaries of Matthew Arnold. Elementary things still need saying. Such terms as "venom," "envy," "malice" and "spite" are, among modern connoisseurs, the staple of appreciation (it is, at any rate, difficult to find anything on Pope in other terms): ". . . we are in the happy position of being able, quite imperturbably, to enjoy the fun. . . . We sit at our ease, reading those *Satires* and *Epistles*, in which the verses, when they were written, resembled nothing so much as spoonfuls of boiling oil, ladled out by a fiendish monkey at an upstairs window upon such of the passers-by whom the wretch had a grudge against—and we are delighted." The Victorians disapproved; Bloomsbury approves: that is the revolution of taste.

It is, in some ways, a pity that we know so much about Pope's life. If nothing had been known but the works, would "envy," "venom," "malice," "spite" and the rest have played so large a part in the commentary? There is, indeed, evidence in the satires of strong personal feelings, but even

—or, rather, especially—where these appear strongest, what (if we are literate) we should find most striking is an intensity of art. To say, with Leslie Stephen and Lytton Strachey, that in the character of Sporus Pope "seems to be actually screaming with malignant fury" is to betray an essential inability to read Pope.

But one has to conclude from published criticism that the nature of Pope's art is very little understood. Just as I reach this point there comes to hand the following, by an American critic: [8] "A familiar charge often brought against Shelley is lack of discipline, but in such charges one must always know what the poet is trying to control. If, as in the case of Pope, it is the mere perfection of a regulated line of verse, the problem becomes one of craftsmanship." A "mere perfection of a regulated line of verse" is not anything as clearly and precisely indicated as the critic, perhaps, supposes; but that he supposes Pope's technique ("craftsmanship" being plainly depreciatory) to be something superficial, some mere skill of arranging a verbal surface, is confirmed by what he goes on to say: Pope's "recitation of the dogmas of his day is hollow," and "in his day as in ours it is a relatively simple matter to accept a ritual of devotion as a substitute for an understanding of basic moral values."

An "understanding of basic moral values" is not a claim one need be concerned to make for a poet, but that Pope's relation to the "basic moral values" of the civilization he belonged to was no mere matter of formal salute and outward deference has been sufficiently shown above, in the discussion of the close of *Epistle IV*. When Pope contemplates the bases and essential conditions of Augustan culture his imagination fires to a creative glow that produces what is poetry even by Romantic standards. His contemplation is religious in its seriousness. The note is that of these lines, which come in *Epistle III* not long

[8] Horace Gregory: *A Defense of Poetry* in *The New Republic* 11th October 1933.

after a vigorous satiric passage and immediately before another:

Ask we what makes one keep and one bestow?
That Pow'r who bids the Ocean ebb and flow,
Bids seed-time, harvest, equal course maintain,
Thro' reconcil'd extremes of drought and rain,
Builds life on Death, on Change Duration founds,
And gives th' eternal wheels to know their rounds.

The order of Augustan civilization evokes characteristically in Pope, its poet, when he is moved by the vision of it, a profound sense of it as dependent on and harmonious with an ultimate and inclusive order. The sense of order expressed in his art when he is at his best (and he is at his best more than most poets) is nothing merely conventional or superficial, explicable in terms of social elegance and a pattern of verse. His technique, concerned as it is with arranging words and "regulating" movements, is the instrument of a fine organization, and it brings to bear pressures and potencies that can turn intense personal feelings into something else. "His 'poetic criticism of life,'" says Lytton Strachey, gibbeting solemn fatuity, "was simply and solely the heroic couplet." Pope would have found it hard to determine what precisely this means, but he certainly would not have found the fatuity Arnold's, and if the Augustan idiom in which he expressed much the same commonplaces as Arnold's differed from the Victorian, it was not in being less solemn.

Ask you what Provocation I have had?
The strong Antipathy of Good to Bad [9]

—we may not accept this as suggesting adequately the moral basis of Pope's satire, but it is significant that Pope could offer such an account: his strength as a satirist was that he lived in an age when such an account could be offered.

The passages of solemnly exalted imagination like those adduced above come with-

[9] *Epilogue to the Satires, Dialogue II.*

out incongruity in the midst of the satire—
the significance of this needs no further insisting on. What does need insisting on is
that with this capacity for poised and subtle variety goes a remarkable command of
varied satiric tones. The politeness of the
Atticus portrait is very different from that
of the *Rape of the Lock* (a work that, in
my opinion, has enjoyed more than justice); the intense destructive vivacity of
the Sporus portrait is different from that of
the attack on Timon; the following (which
is very far from an exception) is enough
to dispose of the judgment that "Pope was
witty but not humorous"—the theme is Paper Credit:

> Had Colepepper's whole wealth been hops and
>   hogs,
> Could he himself have sent it to the dogs?
> His Grace will game: to White's a Bull be led,
> With spurning heels and with a butting head.
> To White's be carry'd, as to ancient games,
> Fair Coursers, Vases, and alluring Dames.
> Shall then Uxurio, if the stakes he sweep,
> Bear home six Whores, and make his Lady
>   weep?

The story of Sir Balaam at the end of
Epistle III is, again, quite different—but
one cannot by enumerating, even if there
were room, do justice to Pope's variety. Indeed, to call attention to the satiric variety
as such is to risk a misleading stress.

Even Mr. Eliot, in *Homage to John Dryden,* manages to limit Pope very unjustly.
Some accidental unfair suggestion one
might expect in such casual reference. But
there is decidedly more than that to com-
plain of.

For instance:

> "But the effect of the portraits of Dryden is to
> transform the object to something greater, as
> were transformed the verses of Cowley quoted
> above.
>
> A fiery soul, which working out its way,
> Fretted the pigmy body to decay:
> And o'er informed the tenement of clay.
>
> These lines are not merely a magnificent tribute.
> They create the object which they contemplate;

the poetry is purer than anything in Pope except
the last lines of the *Dunciad*."

This is a judgment that Matthew Arnold
would have understood—or thought he understood; for one knows that Mr. Eliot is
not appealing here to the prejudices that it
is the general aim of his essay to destroy.
Yet the judgment is perplexing. The end of
the *Dunciad* was admired in the Victorian
age as approaching nearer to "pure poetry"
than Pope does characteristically; but no
one could have better pointed out than Mr.
Eliot its strength and subtlety of wit. The
passage seems to me finer than anything in
Dryden; decidedly finer, for instance, than
the comparable part of *Mac Flecknoe*. It
has a greater intensity (an intensity that
Dryden, with his virtues of good humour
and good nature, was incapable of), and
this is manifest in the very much tauter
and more sensitive verse, the finer life of
the movement.

As for "comic creation," it seems to me
easy to find passages of Pope that have a
like advantage over the lines of Dryden
quoted by Mr. Eliot:

> The country rings around with loud alarms,
> And raw in fields the rude militia swarms;
> Mouths without hands; maintained at vast ex-
>   pense,
> In peace a charge, in war a weak defence;
> Stout once a month, they march, a blust'ring
>   band,
> And ever, but in times of need, at hand;
> This was the morn, when issuing on the guard,
> Drawn up in rank and file they stood prepared
> Of seeming arms to make a short essay,
> Then hasten to be drunk, the business of the
>   day.

Repeated re-readings of both passages only
convince me the more that this of Dryden's
is much inferior to the following, which
starts twenty lines before the final paragraph of the *Dunciad*:

> More had she spoke, but yawn'd—All Nature
>   nods:
> What mortal can resist the Yawn of Gods?
> Churches and Chapels instantly it reach'd;

(St. James's first, for leaden Gilbert preach'd)
Then catch'd the Schools; the Hall scarce kept
    awake;
The Convocation gap'd, but could not speak:
Lost was the Nation's Sense, nor could be
    found,
While the long solemn Unison went round:
Wide, and more wide, it spread o'er all the
    realm;
Ev'n Palinurus nodded at the Helm:
The Vapour mild o'er each Committee crept;
Unfinish'd Treaties in each Office slept;
And Chiefless Armies doz'd out the Campaign;
And Navies yawn'd for Orders on the Main.

Dryden, says Mr. Eliot, "bears a curious antithetical resemblance to Swinburne. Swinburne was also a master of words, but Swinburne's words are all suggestion and no denotation; if they suggest nothing, it is because they suggest too much. Dryden's words, on the other hand, are precise, they state immensely, but their suggestiveness is almost nothing." These lines of Pope seem to me to have all the strength of Dryden's, and to have, in addition, a very remarkable potency of suggestion.

We feel the enveloping, thickening, drowsy vapour spread irresistibly and take on, even, something of a rich romantic glamour—a quality concentrated in

Ev'n Palinurus nodded at the Helm.

This is certainly poetic creation, even by Romantic standards, and yet it is, at the same time, "comic creation." The suggestive richness is blended with something quite un-Romantic:

Lost was the Nation's Sense, nor could be found,
While the long solemn Unison went round.

The effect of the first of these lines is, to nineteenth-century taste, intrinsically unpoetical, but in the second line the "long solemn Unison" is, though ludicrous, at the same time truly solemn. The "Chiefless Armies" doze in an immensely fantastic dream-comedy, and the Navies yawn vastly on an enchanted sea.

Beside the passage of *Mac Flecknoe* in

which Dryden uses Cowley may be set, not to Pope's disadvantage, this from the fourth book of the *Dunciad*:

When Dullness, smiling,—"Thus revive the
    Wits!
But murder first, and mince them all to bits;
As erst Medea (cruel, so to save!)
A new Edition of old Aeson gave;
Let standard-authors, thus, like trophies born,
Appear more glorious as more hack'd and torn.
And you, my Critics! in the chequer'd shade,
Admire new light thro' holes yourselves have
    made.
Leave not a foot of verse, a foot of stone,
A Page, a Grave, that they can call their own."

A commentary like that which Mr. Eliot makes on Dryden's borrowings ("only a poet could have made what Dryden made of them") is applicable to Pope's, except that there seems to be even more point in Pope's use of his, and a greater intensity of surprise in his poetry. The ragged squalor of the Critics in their dark garrets ("batter'd and decay'd") is ironically enhanced by contrast with Milton's

many a youth and many a maid
Dancing in the chequered shade.

But it is the use of Waller that is most felicitous:

The soul's dark cottage, battered and decay'd,
Lets in new light through chinks that Time hath
    made.

There is nothing merely flippant in Pope's sardonic play upon "light"; the solemnity of Waller's theme is present in the indignant observation that it was not Time that made these holes. Indeed, the seriousness of the original is intensified, for Waller is rather easily conventional in his solemn sentiment. The weight makes itself felt in the next couplet, the last of those quoted:

Leave not a foot of verse, a foot of stone,
A Page, a Grave, that they can call their own.

The recognition of inevitable death, decay and oblivion charges the bitterness of this

—of the pun in the first line and the sardonic concentration of the second.

The Metaphysical descent here is plain, but no plainer than in abundance of other passages. The following, in its satiric mode, has in the opening the deep note of those lines in the *Elegy* ("Most souls, 'tis true," etc.), and the ironical fantasy of the whole has a poetic intensity extraordinarily rich in beauty, oddness and surprise:

> The common Soul, of Heaven's more frugal make,
> Serves but to keep fools pert, and knaves awake:
> A drowsy Watchman, that just gives a knock,
> And breaks our rest, to tell us what's a-clock.
> Yet by some object, ev'ry brain is stirr'd;
> The dull may waken to a humming-bird;
> The most recluse, discreetly open'd, find
> Congenial matter in the Cockle-kind;
> The mind, in Metaphysics at a loss,
> May wander in a wilderness of Moss;
> The head that turns at super-lunar things,
> Pois'd with a tail, may steer on Wilkins' wings.

An element that in the close of the *Dunciad* blends with the sublime here associates naturally with quite other effects:

> With that, a Wizard Old his *Cup* extends;
> Which whoso tastes, forgets his former friends,
> Sire, Ancestors, Himself.[10] One casts his eyes
> Up to a *Star*, and like Endymion dies;
> A *Feather*, shooting from another's head,
> Extracts his brain; and Principle is fled;
> Lost is his God, his Country, ev'ry thing;
> And nothing left but Homage to a King!
> The vulgar herd turn off to roll with Hogs,
> To run with Horses, or to hunt with Dogs;

[10] These first two and a half lines, by themselves, would be taken for Tennyson.

> But, sad example! never to escape
> Their Infamy, still keep the human shape.
> But she, good Goddess, sent to ev'ry child
> Firm Impudence, or Stupefaction mild;
> And straight succeeded, leaving shame no room,
> Cibberian forehead, or Cimmerian gloom.

But illustration might go on indefinitely. A representative selection of passages would fill a great many pages. A selection of all Pope that one would wish to have by one for habitual re-reading would fill a great many more. Is it necessary to disclaim the suggestion that he is fairly represented in short extracts? No one, I imagine, willingly reads through the *Essay on Man* (Pope piquing himself on philosophical or theological profundity and acumen is intolerable, and he cannot, as Dryden can, argue interestingly in verse); but to do justice to him one must read through not merely the *Epistles*, but, also as a unit, the fourth book of the *Dunciad*, which I am inclined to think the most striking manifestation of his genius. It is certainly satire, and I know of nothing that demonstrates more irresistibly that satire can be great poetry.

An adequate estimate of Pope would go on to describe the extraordinary key-position he holds, the senses in which he stands between the seventeenth and the eighteenth centuries. Communications from the Metaphysicals do not pass beyond him; he communicates forward, not only with Johnson, but also (consider, for instance, *Eloïsa to Abelard*) with Thomson and Gray. It was not for nothing that he was so interested in Milton.

George Sherburn

The *Dunciad,* Book IV

THE last poem that Pope wrote was probably the fourth Book of the *Dunciad*, and for a poet whose art was always marked by control, a last poem should be at least among his best. Yet Joseph Warton and others have thought this Book an "unhappy" addition to the poem; and in recent years, when commentators have agreed in preferring the 1729 version of the *Dunciad* to that of 1743, there has been danger that we may casually seem to undervalue the merits of Book IV—which, unlike Books I–III, is obviously not in competition with an earlier version. It may be permissible, consequently, to examine again the diverse complexity of the Book in such detail as will enable us at least to see its true nature.

First, we may consider its intellectual quality. If the reader is one of those who think intellectual poetry a contradiction in terms, he clearly need read no further here; for to the present writer it seems true that to read Book IV without regarding it as an intellectual pronouncement is to miss the greater part of its power. Pope, as Warton remarked with high praise, "chose to be *the poet of reason*," and the statement is true, even if it is necessary to realize that reason was a word of varying implications in Pope's day.

Professor Sutherland has called attention to the fact [1] that two hundred lines of this Book derive from Pope's project for a poetical essay on education, and certainly education in at least lines 138–336 is a fea-

tured topic. Pope covers the whole field from the time when the boy-senator is flogged for dull memory work ill done to the glorious moment when the finished fop returns from the "educational" grand tour. The schools, Pope alleges, padlock the mind rather than open it; and the university wastes time on logic and metaphysics, subjects so pedantic and impractical as to make it easy for the student to be unaware of "Civil Duties" and to believe contentedly in the doctrine so dear to Dulness—

The Right Divine of Kings to govern wrong!

The passage devoted to the universities is memorable for the eloquent and dramatic episode (lines 203–74) involving Pope's old enemy Richard Bentley, who died, aged eighty, about four months after the lines appeared in print. Though perhaps the most personal of all the satire in Book IV, these lines are typical of the development away from mere personality to a wider meaning. Pope, it is clear, had slight grounds for a personal hatred of Bentley: his dislike was consistently for the slashing dryasdust scholarship the man exemplified. Depiction of personal traits, however, is marked in this passage—in Bentley's tempestuous academic career, his love of port, his brusque, awful manner as well as in the manipulations of his hat; but, what is far more important, Bentley is made chiefly the effective symbol of the fact that

The critic Eye, that microscope of Wit,
Sees hairs and pores, examines bit by bit—

and, thus microscopically focused, will never comprehend larger and nobler issues.

[1] *The Poems of Alexander Pope* (Twickenham ed.), V (1943), xxxi. Unless otherwise specified all textual quotations from the *Dunciad* are from this edition, by Professor James R. Sutherland.

Reprinted from *Studies in English 1944*, Austin, Texas, University of Texas Press, 1945, pp. 174–190, by permission of the author and the publisher.

Pope is still blind to the real if humble uses of technical literary scholarship, but its dangers he perceives and expresses with immortal trenchancy. His sense of the seriousness of these dangers transcends and dignifies his prolonged animus against Bentley. The satire here is not intellectual merely because it is about scholarship: it is creditably based on respectable intellectual principles.

In keeping with his usual method of arranging sequences of episodes in contrasting moods or tones, Pope passes from the friends of Aristotle (Bentley and the other dons) to the travelled fops and virtuosi, and then reverts to more intellectual matters in his condemnation of free-thinkers. His fashionable travellers are castigated for their vapidity, and they illustrate the failings inherent in the "Cibberian forehead," as Bentley and Dr. Clarke illustrate the "Cimmerian gloom" of dark intellectuality (line 532). Pope's travellers and virtuosi tend to be obscurely pseudonymous. Paridel, Annius, Pollio, and Mummius are all uncertainly identified or not at all. The point again is that here finally the poet is more concerned with fashionable follies than with individual fools. The elegant specialists, or virtuosi, are to Pope the sort of men who, if they do not imagine reason given them "but to study *flies*," certainly

> See Nature in some partial narrow shape,
> And let the Author of the Whole escape:
> Learn but to trifle; or, who most observe,
> To wonder at their Maker, not to serve.

Thus they answer the wishes of Dulness, who hopes to see literary learning, awareness of civil duties, and the investigation of nature, all extinguished by a devotion to miscellaneous and unmeaning factual detail or by intricate and ultimately perplexing logical complexities. Such is the burden of Pope's satiric comment on education.

His remarks about free-thinkers must surprise those who insist that the author of the *Essay on Man* was himself at heart a deist. One is, of course, tempted to explain his attacks (lines 459–516) on "rationalizing divines" (as Fielding loved to call them) and on other heterodox or skeptical persons as due to the influence of his new adviser, Warburton. But, at least briefly, in the earlier forms of the *Dunciad*, before he knew Warburton, Pope had paid his respects to Anthony Collins, Toland, Tindal, and Woolston,[2] and the evidence is fairly conclusive that he was early eager in his scorn of free-thinkers. Here in *Dunciad* IV he attacks not merely such men as Tindal and Thomas Gordon ("Silenus"), but he is glancing at more important personages. One is, presumably, Dr. Samuel Clarke, who promoted argument over the divine attributes and also expounded the theological ideas of Sir Isaac Newton. Writing in a period when the empiricism of Locke made attacks on "high priori" metaphysics fashionable, Pope naturally fell into the confusions of his day. Clarke had been blamed for the alleged heterodoxy of Queen Caroline, and while it is improbable that his "reasoning downward" made him "doubt of God," more people than Pope and Bolingbroke believed him a doubter. His method of reasoning was quite contrary to the spirit of Locke's work. Pope evidently preferred this new empiricism; for he has his "gloomy clerk" say scornfully:

> Let others creep by timid steps, and slow,
> On plain Experience lay foundations low,
> By common sense to common knowledge bred,
> And last, to Nature's Cause thro' Nature led.
> All-seeing in thy mists, we want no guide,
> Mother of Arrogance, and Source of Pride!
> We nobly take the high Priori Road,
> And reason downward, till we doubt of God:
> Make Nature still incroach upon his plan;
> And shove him off as far as e'er we can:
> Thrust some Mechanic Cause into his place;
> Or bind in Matter, or diffuse in Space,
> Or, at one bound o'er-leaping all his laws,
> Make God Man's Image, Man the final Cause,
> Find Virtue local, all Relation scorn,

[2] *Ed. cit.*, V, 144–5, 174–5.

> See all in *Self*, and but for self be born:
> Of nought so certain as our *Reason* still,
> Of nought so doubtful as of *Soul* and *Will*.

Dr. Clarke, however, was also an experimental scientist, and his position (if indeed it is surely intended for his) is somewhat misrepresented. Since Bolingbroke and Warburton both apparently disliked Clarke's metaphysics, it is impossible to determine if either or both here influenced Pope; but it is obvious that the poet intended to be on the side of the angels and at the same time to shun metaphysical or "misty" thinking.

A famous passage from Shaftesbury's *Characteristics* also meets Pope's disapprobation here. Other passages from the work had given inspiration for parts of the *Essay on Man*; but in *Dunciad* IV the "sweet enthusiasm" of Theocles ("The Moralists"), which identified Nature with Deity, is reprehended in one couplet (487–8) and in a long footnote doubtless partly due to Warburton. The passage might seem a further defense against the charge of Spinozism or fatalism made against the *Essay on Man*, but in any case it is an attack on fashionable heterodoxy or deism.[3] Probably Shaftesbury's "extravagancy" and Platonic apriorism annoyed Pope—and Bolingbroke, who also silently borrowed from *Characteristics*—more than did many specific doctrinal statements.

Throughout this part of *Dunciad* IV Pope is, of course, making an anti-rational appeal to common sense as an antidote to the metaphysics of rationalizing divines or deists. He opposes also all limited "microscopic" technical study as well as the follies of travellers and elegant virtuosi. Both "folly's cup" and "wisdom's grave disguise" are scourged. Education fails because the pupil is made

> First slave to Words, then vassal to a Name,
> Then dupe to Party; child and man the same;
> Bounded by Nature, narrow'd still by Art,
> A trifling head, and a contracted heart.

What Pope commends is the humanly sympathetic and "open" mind actuated by judgment and common sense: what he disapproves are metaphysics, the superficial follies of the wealthy, and the microscopic scholarship of men such as Bentley, Kuster, Burman, and Wasse. These scholars are mentioned by name, as are leading freethinkers or theologians of the time. Concerning the virtuosi Pope is pseudonymously coy; but clearly his gallery of dunces is well filled and includes a rich assortment of all kinds. Poets and painters get off easily in this Book, and although Italian opera is ridiculed, we have in lines 65–70 the most famous and most timely compliment ever paid to Handel.[4]

So much for the intellectual content of the poem; its imaginative quality may be considered in two aspects—the structure of the Book as a whole and the specific quality of individual images.

The structural pattern of Book IV seems at first sight more original, less in the heroic tradition, than were the devices of the earlier Books. Book I derived from *MacFlecknoe* and other sources; Book II, echoing the funeral games for Anchises (*Aeneid* V), and Book III, drawing from the prophetic visions of *Aeneid* VI and *Paradise Lost* XI and XII, seem perhaps more normal for a mock epic. Book IV presents a grand drawing-room, appropriate for a royal birthday, at which titles or orders of

---

[3] One must suspect from a curious footnote to the *Essay on Man*, Ep. II, l. 165 ff., as found in the quarto edition of 1743, p. 16, that Pope was somewhat confused in his attitude towards *Characteristics*. Relevant also is the note to *Dunciad* IV, 244, and of course one finds much in Paul Vater's *Pope und Shaftesbury* (Halle, 1897).

[4] The great composer was, when Pope wrote these lines, bankrupt and in Ireland—producing among other things *Messiah*. He so appreciated Pope's praise that in his next opera (*Semele*, 1743) he inserted in Congreve's libretto the famous aria, "Where'er you walk"—set to the words of Pope's *Summer*, lines 73–6.

merit are bestowed by the Queen of Dulness. The scene is chiefly that of such a drawing-room, but it unfolds in a slightly confusing dreamlike fashion into an academic meeting for the conferring of degrees. This latter aspect of the scene intrigued both Pope and Warburton, not merely because the *Dunciad* was a satire on pedantry, but because in 1741 both Pope and Warburton had been proposed for the LL.D. at Oxford, and since the grace was not voted for Warburton, Pope declined it for himself. They were both unusually "degree-conscious" at the time the poem was finished.

Book IV has been thought confused in structure; but there were special reasons why its pattern of action was easily grasped in the early 'forties. Henry Fielding in two or three very popular farces had shown royal levees crammed with incongruous episodes that followed each other kaleidoscopically much as do the passages of Book IV. And it may be added that in these plays and elsewhere in the 'thirties Fielding perhaps did more to ripen Cibber's fame in satire and make him eligible for the laureateship of Dulness than anyone else—Cibber himself excepted. When Cibber wrote his famous *Letter to Mr. Pope, Inquiring into the MOTIVES that might induce him in his Satyrical Works, to be so frequently fond of Mr. Cibber's Name* (1742), he might more appropriately have addressed his inquiry to Fielding [5] if his concern in the matter was, so to speak, disinterested; but Cibber in 1742 foresaw an attack by Pope in the making, and what Pope said at that moment mattered more than what Fielding had been incessantly saying for ten years.

As models for his projected Book IV Fielding furnished Pope two or three scenes from royal drawing-rooms. In the *Author's Farce* (1730) he had scored with an uproarious scene from the drawing-

room of Queen Nonsense, and in 1736 *Pasquin* showed as rival queens Common Sense and Ignorance, and the drawing-room of Queen Ignorance was as confused and delightfully heterogeneous as a bear-garden. In his *Historical Register for 1736* an episode in Act III shows "Apollo in a great chair, surrounded by attendants" and casting the parts *à la* Cibber for Shakespeare's *King John*. Probably not Fielding's (and certainly not Hesiod Cooke's) was a piece of similar structure, called *The Battle of the Poets; or, The Contention for the Laurel,* which was very briefly inserted in the second act of *Tom Thumb* just before Cibber was made laureate. A scene with a foolish king or a mock queen or goddess enthroned makes an admirable focal point about which farcical episode may loosely revolve. These plays by Fielding were enormously popular, and they almost certainly gave form to the new Book of the *Dunciad.* Doubtless authors other than Fielding anticipated Pope in the use of this scene, but no other author at the time had prepared Pope's public for the device as had Henry Fielding.

Not merely the structure of these farcical drawing-rooms but also the individual episodes in them bear some relation to Book IV. In the *Author's Farce* Fielding is ridiculing the irrational theater of his day, and he introduces many more types of amusement than Pope presents; but he introduces types and persons notable in the *Dunciad,* such as Pantomime (whose capers resemble those of Mad Mathesis), Novel (Eliza Haywood), Orator Henley, Count Ugly (Heidegger), and Opera. Fielding's contest for the bays in this farce is won by Opera. Sir Farcical Comic in the first form of the play thereupon sings his lament, and thus puts Nonsense to sleep, much as in *Dunciad* II the reading contest had been soporific. The song is one of Fielding's neatest absurdities concerning Cibber. In a preface to the *Provok'd Husband* (1728) Cibber had murdered the king's English in several ways that Field-

[5] Practically all of Fielding's attacks on Cibber are treated in Houghton W. Taylor's "Fielding upon Cibber" (*MP*, XXIX [1931], 73–90).

ing never forgot.[6] Among other things he had misspelled *paraphernalia*. Hence when the disappointed Sir Farcical (i.e., Cibber) sings Nonsense to sleep, it is with the reproachful lines:

> Can my Goddess then forget
>   *Paraphonalia*
>   *Paraphonalia*
> Can she the Crown on another Head set,
>   Than of her *Paraphonalia?*

The action throughout this puppet-show episode is thoroughly farcical and confusedly noisy; but the visible action made the shifting "turns" easier to grasp than they would be in a non-dramatic poem.

In *Pasquin* (1736) Fielding is still dealing in "Dunciad" material. Theology, law, and physic, all fail Queen Common Sense, and presently she is told that

> Queen Ignorance is landed in your realm,
> With a vast power from Italy and France
> Of singers, fiddlers, tumblers, and rope-dancers.

Eventually Common Sense is killed by her Priest, and Ignorance settles herself to rule with the plaudits of the Royal Society, Grub-street, the learned professions, Harlequin, and the opera; but they are all frightened off stage by the sudden appearance of the mere ghost of Common Sense. The thinking, again, seems much influenced by the 1729 *Dunciad*, and possibly it is prophetic in some respects of *Dunciad* IV.

At any rate the structural pattern of this last *Dunciad* had been made familiar to the world of fashion by Fielding's popular farces. The pictorial effect of a spurious goddess enthroned with symbolic attendants grouped grotesquely and statuesquely near by and with different groups of "sub-

jects" passing in (satiric) review before the goddess would not perplex the imaginations of those who had been among the "fashionable mobs" who had attended the little theater in the Haymarket before the crisis of 1737. The episodic unfolding of Fielding's farces and Pope's Book IV are also somewhat similar, and, finally, both writers were satirists with a particular fondness for the low "Cibberian forehead." [7]

It is probable that Pope, who habitually composed in episodic fragments, may have written parts of Book IV before he adopted the royal drawing-room as a device for loose unification. We have his remark to Spence about "an Essay on Education; part of which I have inserted in the *Dunciad*," [8] and at the point (line 138) where the inserted section begins, there is some wavering in the transitions. After the stage is set, Opera in the first abrupt episode petitions for the silencing of Handel. There follows a curious passage (73–80) that states Pope's strong and sincere concept of the positive attractive power of dulness

---

[6] Cibber's "To the Reader," where most of his blunders occur, is dated January 27, 1727/8, but the printed version appeared in time for Pope to make last-minute insertions from it in his "Peri Bathous," which was on sale March 8. The newspapers seized upon the errors before that date, but Pope must have responded instantly to this preface; Fielding responded perpetually.

[7] It has been thought (W. L. Cross, *History of Henry Fielding*, I, 132–4) that Pope and Fielding were not friendly; but there seems to be no reason for such an assumption apart from the attacks of the *Grub-street Journal* on Fielding's plays. These had nothing to do with Pope. Richard Russell, editor of the *Journal*, was a friend of Jeremy Collier, and early in his *Journal* he had announced his intention of continuing Collier's war upon theatrical immorality and profaneness. This aim easily embroiled Russell with Fielding. Pope and Fielding were both friends of Ralph Allen and of the Earl of Chesterfield, and, in an unpublished letter to Allen, Pope mentions Fielding as at least an acquaintance. A copy of *Joseph Andrews* still exists that Pope had bound up in his favorite red morocco and gave to Ann Arbuthnot. Fielding in turn filled his writings with high compliments to Pope. Ten weeks after the *New Dunciad* appeared in 1742 Fielding and William Young ("Parson Adams") published a translation of *Plutus the God of Riches*, the footnotes of which attacked Theobald in a way that must have delighted Pope. In choosing their dunces and their friends Pope and Fielding were accidentally or consciously "of a mind."

[8] Spence, *Anecdotes* (ed. Singer, 1820), p. 315.

for the many who instinctively swarm about the goddess "conglob'd" like bees "about their dusky Queen." These "naturally dull," a footnote explains, are followed by the involuntarily dull, and by a third group that are accidentally or temporarily dull. By the time we reach line 101 the movement of these attendants has clarified and become in some sort processional—

> There march'd the bard and blockhead, side by side.

And the stately stride of Montalto (Hanmer) is succeeded by the more vigorous march of Bentley (lines 203 ff.), who in turn gives way to the travelled fops (line 275). These successive groups, we are told in line 136, are

> Each eager to present the first Address.

But in the section on education that immediately follows no petitions are presented. We have the early petition of Opera, and thereafter none until the lac'd Governor naturally ends his presentation of his foppish young traveller and the imported mistress (lines 282–335) with a request for acceptance and protection. Annius follows at once with a petition for aid in his numismatical "cheating," and he is opposed by Mummius. So likewise the petition of the expert in carnations is opposed by the lover of butterflies. On the whole, one must conclude, the poet is preoccupied with description of the grotesque and miscellaneous court rather than with a rehearsal of petitions: he seeks diversity of episode fully as much as he does structural unity of the whole. This tendency, in spite of all the learned have said, is quite typical of English neo-classicism, and in this as in most of Pope's poems episodes follow loosely in diverse and contrasting moods, just as in a suite by Purcell or Handel an allegro is followed by an andante or a courante by a rigadoon.

In all these contrasting episodes is apparent a rich variety in the nature of individual images, a variety which is the immediate and chief source of appeal in the poem. At the start of any consideration of these it must be recognized that it is erroneous to think that Pope is deficient in concrete, highly specific imagery. His theory is not that of "general effects secured through general details," though that may have been the method of Sir Joshua Reynolds and other reputable theorists. Pope's most significant comment on the matter is found in the note to his *Iliad*, Book VI, line 595 (1716), concerning the farewell of Hector to his infant son Astyanax:

There never was a finer Piece of Painting than this. *Hector* extends his Arms to embrace his Child: the Child affrighted at the glittering of his Helmet and the shaking of the Plume, shrinks backward to the Breast of his Nurse; *Hector* unbraces his Helmet, lays it on the Ground, takes the Infant in his Arms, lifts him towards Heaven, and offers a Prayer for him to the Gods: then returns him to the Mother *Andromache*, who receives him with a Smile of Pleasure, but at the same instant the Fears for her Husband make her burst into Tears. All these are but small Circumstances, but so artfully chosen, that every Reader immediately feels the force of them, and represents the whole in the utmost Liveliness to his Imagination. This alone might be a Confutation of that false Criticism some have fallen into, who affirm that a Poet ought only to collect the great and noble Particulars in his Paintings. But it is in the Images of Things as in the Characters of Persons; where a small Action, or even a small Circumstance of an Action, lets us more into the Knowledge and Comprehension of them, than the material and principal Parts themselves. As we find this in a History, so we do in a Picture, where sometimes a small Motion or Turning of a Finger will express the Character and Action of the Figure more than all the other Parts of the Design. *Longinus* indeed blames an Author's insisting too much on trivial Circumstances; but in the same Place extols *Homer* as "the Poet who best knew how to make use of important and beautiful Circumstances, and to avoid the mean and superfluous ones." There is a vast difference betwixt a *small* Circumstance and a *trivial* one, and the smallest become important if they are well chosen, and not confused.

Himself a painter, Pope knew the value of a vivid phrase; he recognizes clearly the imaginative power of the highly specific, "small" detail. It is true that in *Dunciad* IV many minute details do not now come truly to life without the aid of annotation. Editors have done much, but the topical nature of satire still causes the casual reader perplexity.

A *Feather* shooting from another's head,
Extracts his brain, and Principle is fled—

is a curious way of suggesting that the plume worn by Knights of the Garter takes from the members of that order all principle except "Homage to a King." Similarly Pope's terse manner of saying (lines 533–6) that Self-conceit is a mirror which shows us to ourselves subjectively transformed into "Patriot, Chief, or Saint"—or what we will—requires study. The poem abounds in difficult details drawn from specialized techniques such as then belonged, for example, to the amateur of carnations:

Soft on the paper ruff its leaves I spread,
Bright with the gilded button tipt its head.

Professor Sutherland has been admirably illuminating on these lines, but the "gilded button" is perhaps still somewhat too much involved in the mystery of the florist's hotbeds. Other instances of Pope's technical "learning" may be found in the various details (e.g., lines 549–65) that come from culinary arts. In many such passages Pope's imagery seems as "far-fetched" and specialized as that of his great predecessor —and in some sense master—John Donne.

This is a point to realize. Pope may be deficient in the conventional images of poetry—those drawn from nature or from such inspiring universals as love or death— but from first to last his satires are full of images that might occur to a modern realistic painter or poet. The French cook, "a Priest succinct in amice white," would be merely a perfect "Dutch piece" if Pope had not added the symbolism that elevates the gourmet's cult to a religious level, by means of the amice, the "copious Sacrifice," and the dubious devotion due

To three essential Partridges in one.

Pope recurs repeatedly to food-metaphors; a good example is lines 227–32 of Bentley's speech:

For Attic Phrase in Plato let them seek,
I poach in Suidas for unlicens'd Greek.
In ancient Sense if any needs will deal,
Be sure I give them Fragments, not a Meal;
What Gellius or Stobaeus hash'd before,
Or chew'd by blind old Scholiasts o'er and o'er.

These lines are typical of the vivifying use to which Pope can put metaphors in debasing intellectual matters that meet his contempt. Frequently his technical images are purely descriptive rather than (as in Bentley's speech) prejudicial. Take, for example, the intellectually apt couplet:

Like buoys, that never sink into the flood,
On Learning's surface we but lie and nod.

This is fair evidence of observation on the part of a poet whose sea-faring included only voyages on the Thames and one crossing to the Isle of Wight. We may be less content with his ingenuity in meaning when he writes

See! still thy own, the heavy Canon roll,
And Metaphysic smokes involve the Pole.

He may mean simply that the heavy artillery (of metaphysics) is always on the side of Dulness; but from his footnotes one must assume that he expects some Canon of Christ Church, Oxford, to feel that the smoke encircles a paranomasiac poll!

Less ingenious but more biting is such a picture as that of the complete exquisite, Paridel—

Stretch'd on the rack of a too easy chair;

or the picture of the "bowzy Sire," Thomas Gordon, less elegant in its informality. He

shook from out his Pipe the seeds of fire;
Then snapt his box, and strok'd his belly down:
Rosy and rev'rend, tho' without a Gown.
Bland and familiar to the throne he came,
Led up the Youth, and call'd the Goddess
Dame.

In these somewhat "homely" images Pope
is at his best when dealing with mankind;
but he is not limited, and describes the
crafty Annius in rural terms:

Soft, as the wily Fox is seen to creep,
Where bask on sunny banks the simple sheep,
Walk round and round, now prying here, now
there;
So he; but pious, whisper'd first his pray'r.

The poet brings to all this sort of thing a
firm hand and an unerring line—to borrow
his own graphic phrase—but he does not
altogether limit himself to "Dutch" realism. The grand tour of his fop leads to a
satiric gilding of the Italian lily that ad-
vertises the poet's skill in metrics and in
lush detail of artificial loveliness. The fop
was guided

To happy Convents, bosom'd deep in vines,
Where slumber Abbots, purple as their wines:
To Isles of fragrance, lilly-silver'd vales,
Diffusing languor in the panting gales:
To lands of singing, or of dancing slaves,
Love-whisp'ring woods, and lute-resounding
waves.

Such imagery is pleasing but perhaps
obvious. To see that Pope's imagination is
operating subtly throughout the poem one
may wisely consider the appropriate physical movements that vivify and characterize
the dull as they pass the throne of the goddess. Opera, the first, is

a Harlot form soft sliding by,
With mincing step, small voice, and languid
eye

.   .   .   .

By singing Peers up-held on either hand,
She tripp'd and laugh'd, too pretty much to
stand.

Compare this with Sir Thomas Hanmer,
the long-since Speaker of the House of
Commons, come to present to Dulness his
edition of Shakespeare:

There mov'd Montalto with superior air;
His stretch'd-out arm display'd a Volume fair;
Courtiers and Patriots in two ranks divide,
Thro' both he pass'd, and bow'd from side to
side:
But as in graceful act, with awful eye
Compos'd he stood, bold Benson thrust him by:
On two unequal crutches propt he came,
Milton's on this, on that one Johnston's name.
The decent Knight retir'd with sober rage,
Withdrew his hand, and clos'd the pompous
page.

After Sir Thomas

crowds on crowds around the Goddess press,
Each eager to present the first Address.

And among these were the university dons
led by Richard Bentley:

Before them march'd that awful Aristarch;
Plow'd was his front with many a deep Remark:
His Hat, which never vail'd to human pride,
Walker with rev'rence took, and lay'd aside.
Low bow'd the rest: He, kingly, did but nod;
So upright Quakers please both Man and God.

After Bentley's address, not decently wait-
ing its termination,

In flow'd at once a gay embroider'd race,
And titt'ring push'd the Pedants off the
place. . . .

This marks a decline in vigorous movement, a decline that appropriately leads to
the universal yawn. Paridel's relaxation is
followed by the bowzy snoring of Silenus
(Gordon): the diminuendo is now (line
493) marked, but throughout the Book the
movement of the actors on Pope's stage is
living and appropriate. He sees them move,
and makes them visible to us.

Beauty is not the province of satire; and
Pope's poem is not rich in pretty or allur-
ing detail: realism, vigor, incisiveness are
what we expect here—and find. The best
couplet about the fop, for example, comes
when, newly exported from the university,
he begins his travels:

Intrepid then, o'er seas and lands he flew:
Europe he saw, and Europe saw him too.

In Italy and France he

Try'd all *hors-d'oeuvres*, all *liquers* defin'd,
Judicious drank, and greatly-daring din'd.

Obviously still in 1742 Pope has a perfect mastery of satiric epithet! The poet is altogether impartial: he castigates the pedant as neatly as he does the fop. Among the jewels in Bentley's speech to Dulness come, reset from Theobald's words in the earlier form of Book I, the following lines:

For thee we dim the eyes, and stuff the head
With all such reading as was never read:
For thee explain a thing till all men doubt it,
And write about it, Goddess, and about it:
So spins the silk-worm small its slender store,
And labours till it clouds itself all o'er.

One sees here again the steady aim and the sure fire, the language of real life controlled and for its purpose perfect.

And so it seems permissible to borrow Dryden's words from a better occasion and cry out, "Here is God's plenty." There is not the Chaucerian humanity, but there is a humanity that Chaucer would understand and approve, and there is a richness of expressive detail drawn from the most extreme vocations, both aristocratic and proletarian, such as Pope achieved practically nowhere else in the same degree. And Pope's sense of intellectual values, expressed many times in his career, he here restates with a solemn sincerity and a relative lack of personal animus that is fitting in a final poetic achievement. This solemnity is seen in the opening lines and in the famous conclusion. Even critics who insist that true poetry must be either sublime or

pathetic, and who consequently give Pope a low rating, are reconciled to the dignity, sweep, and profound emotion embodied in these last lines. They have been repeatedly praised for their true Longinian sublimity. It is well to remember that in the opinion of Longinus sublimity came from the mind. Book IV of the *Dunciad* is so crammed with extremely diverse imagery that Joseph Warton, for example, thought it "one of the most motley compositions, that, perhaps, is anywhere to be found in the works of so exact a writer as Pope." [9]

But to leave the poem at that is a gross undervaluation both of Pope's organizing design—whether from Fielding or not—and, above all, of the basic integrity of his sense of intellectual values. Pope has a just prejudice against the dunce as an intellectual vacuum as well as against the dunce "with loads of learned lumber in his head." The fourth Book is not a contradiction of the first three Books: it is a richer and more imaginative restatement of the values announced in 1728 and 1729. For once Bowles was right about a poem by Pope when he wrote at the end of his introduction to Book IV:

In polished and pointed satire, in richness of versification and imagery, and in the happy introduction of characters, episodes, figures, and every sort of poetical ornament, adapted to the subject, this book yields, in my opinion, to none of Pope's writings of the same kind.[10]

ADDENDUM: For further "Literary Backgrounds to Book Four of the *Dunciad*" see Aubrey Williams, *PMLA*, LXVIII (1953), 806–13.—G. S.

[9] Warton, *Essays on the Genius and Writings of Pope* (Fifth edition, 1806), II, 369.

[10] Pope's *Works* (ed. William Lisle Bowles, 1806), V, 258.

Maynard Mack

The Muse of Satire

IT GROWS plainer every year that literary study in our part of the twentieth century has been very considerably stimulated by one important event. This event is the gradual reëmergence of rhetoric—by which I mean the reëmergence of a number of interpretive skills and assumptions about literature that under the name of rhetoric once formed part of the medieval trivium and together with grammar made up a study somewhat resembling what we now call literary explication. As we begin the second half of the century, the signs of this rhetorical quickening seem to me to be multiplying very fast.

To begin with a whimsical example, I notice that my reprint of Puttenham's "Arte of English Poesie" (1589), frequently on loan to students, is well thumbed chiefly at the twelve chapters where the rhetorical figures are named and illustrated. Forty-five years ago, when Gregory Smith reprinted Puttenham in his collection of "Elizabethan Critical Essays," these were precisely the chapters, and the only chapters, he chose to leave out. This is a straw in the wind from readers.

There is ampler evidence from writers. One might cite, at the level of research, the speedy proliferation of studies dealing with aspects of rhetorical history: investigations like J. W. H. Atkins' of classical, medieval, and Renaissance criticism, or T. W. Baldwin's of Shakespeare's grammar school training, or Miss Tuve's of sixteenth-century rhetorical manuals. At the level of practical criticism, one could point to the reappearance of rhetorical concepts in literary discourse. One hears the word *de-corum* used nowadays without a sneer; one comes across mentions, though as yet no illuminating discussions, of the "three styles"—high, middle, and low; one even hears the admission that there may be something in genre: "Paradise Lost," Mr. C. S. Lewis has been trying to persuade us, is what it is at least as much because it is a *heroic* poem as because it was written by John Milton.

But doubtless the climactic evidence at the critical level is the so-called—the so ineptly called—"new" criticism. The enormous influence of this body of writing can only be properly understood, I think, if we realize that it has been the pioneering phase—that is to say, the most applied and "practical" phase—in a general revival of rhetorical interests and disciplines. Evoked by the absence of a continuing tradition of rhetorical analysis (for the classical tradition was unfortunately discredited by the time the new critics began to write), this criticism has been an effort, often fumbling, often brilliant, to recapture some of the older exegetical skills, or at any rate to formulate their equivalents, for modern use.

Now rhetoric being a body of learning that insists on the recognition of artifice, one of the effects of its renascence is bound to be the reinvigoration of our sense of distinctions between art and life. If we compare ourselves with the nineteenth century in this respect, we realize that we no longer write, or care to read, books like Mrs. Cowden Clarke's on "The Girlhood of Shakespeare's Heroines" (1850–2); nor do we care to inquire, even with so great a critic as A. C. Bradley, where Hamlet was when

Reprinted by permission from the *Yale Review*, XLI (1951), 80–92.

his father was being murdered, or with Ellen Terry, how the Boy in Henry V learned French: "Did he learn to speak the lingo from Prince Hal, or from Falstaff in London, or did he pick it up during his few weeks in France with the army?" We realize, too, that unlike the nineteenth century we can no longer speak of Shakespeare's "Dark Period" or his "Joyous Comedies," except by enclosing the words in quotation marks. We acknowledge, to be sure, that a playwright and his plays are involved with each other in important ways, but we are much too conscious of artifice to be willing to risk a direct reading from comedy or tragedy to the author's states of mind.

In our dealings with the drama, in fact, most of us are now willing to add to the study of how a work grows or what it does the study of what it is. Inquiries into biographical and historical origins, or into effects on audiences and readers, can and should be supplemented, we are beginning to insist, by a third kind of inquiry treating the work with some strictness as a rhetorical construction: as a "thing made," which, though it reaches backward to an author and forward to an audience, has its artistic identity in between—in the realm of artifice and artifact. With respect to drama, there has lately been building a valuable even if by no means uniformly sound criticism of this kind. But outside the drama, and a few other areas recently invaded, we cannot point to very much. On the subject of poetry in general, Mr. Ricardo Quintana has complained, most of our commentary still "turns out to be either description of our impressions" (i.e., effects), "or reconstruction—largely imaginary—of a precise moment in the poet's emotional history with which we have chosen to equate the poem" (i.e., origins).

One need not share Mr. Quintana's doubt as to the effectiveness of other approaches to feel that in the case of satire, at any rate, what is desperately needed today is inquiry that deals neither with ori-

gins nor effects, but with artifice. Criticism of satiric literature has barely begun to budge from the position of Macaulay, Elwin, Leslie Stephen—all of whom seem, at one time or another, to have regarded it as a kind of dark night of the soul (dank with poisonous dews) across which squibs of envy, malice, hate, and spite luridly explode. Here is a sample from 1880, referring to Pope's "Sporus": "that infusion of personal venom"; "the poet is writing under some bitter mortification"; he is "trying with concentrated malice to sting his adversary"; he is "a tortured victim screaming out the shrillest taunts at his tormentor" (Sir Leslie Stephen). Here is a sample from 1925, referring to Pope's epistles and satires in general: at the time of their creation, "they resembled nothing so much as spoonsful of boiling oil, ladled out by a fiendish monkey at an upstairs window upon such of the passers-by whom the wretch had a grudge against" (Lytton Strachey). And here is a sample from 1941, referring to the "Dunciad"—if anything the tone is shriller: "impossible to admire it without an unenviable pleasure in sheer spite"; "the tone of furious indiscriminate hatred"; "the half-crazed misanthropy of the whole poem"; "a general indictment of the human race"; "this universal shriek of loathing and despair" (Gilbert Highet).

In this essay, I should like to ventilate this fetid atmosphere a little by opening a window on one or two rhetorical observations. These observations will be commonplaces, but the record suggests that they can bear repetition. My illustrations will be drawn from Pope, especially from his formal satires, such as the "Epistle to Dr. Arbuthnot"; and my thesis will be that even in these apparently very personal poems, we overlook what is most essential if we overlook the distinction between the historical Alexander Pope and the dramatic Alexander Pope who speaks them.

It is to underscore this distinction that I have ventured in my title to name the

Muse. For the Muse ought always to be our reminder that it is not the author as man who casts these shadows on our printed page, but the author as poet: an instrument possessed by and possessing—Plato would have said a god, we must at any rate say an art. And, moreover, the Muse ought to remind us that in any given instance the shadow may not delineate even the whole poet, but perhaps only that angle of his sensibility which best refracts the light from epic, elegy, pastoral, lyric, satire. The fact is not without significance, it seems to me, that though Pope, following the great victories of naturalism in the seventeenth century, had to make do with a minimum of mythology and myth, he never discarded the Muse, either the conception or the term. She appears with remarkable regularity even in his satires, and there, for my present purposes, I am choosing to regard her as a not entirely playful symbol of the impersonality of the satiric genre— of its rhetorical and dramatic character.

Rhetorically considered, satire belongs to the category of *laus et vituperatio*, praise and blame. It aims, like all poetry, in Sidney's phrase, through the "fayning notable images of vertues [and] vices," to achieve "that delightful teaching which must be the right describing note to know a Poet by." And it has, of course, its own distinctive means to this. Prominent among them to a casual eye is the *exemplum* in the form of portrait, like Dryden's Zimri, or Pope's Atticus; and the middle style, which stresses conversational speech (more than passion or grandiloquence) along with aphoristic phrasings, witty turns, and ironical indirections. Less prominent but more important than either of these is the satiric fiction into which such materials must be built.

All good satire, I believe it is fair to say, exhibits an appreciable degree of fictionality. Where the fiction inheres in familiar elements like plot, as in "Absalom and Achitophel" or "The Rape of the Lock" or "The Dunciad" or "The Beggar's Opera,"

its presence is, of course, unmistakable; and it is unmistakable, too, in such satires as Swift's "Argument against Abolishing Christianity" or his "Modest Proposal," where the relation of the speaker to the author is extremely oblique, not to say antithetical. But when the relation is only slightly oblique, as in Pope's formal satires, the fictionality takes subtler forms and resides in places where, under the influence of romantic theories of poetry as the spontaneous overflow of powerful emotions, we have become unaccustomed to attend to it. (How far unaccustomed is seen if we reflect that the extraordinary views of Gulliver in Houyhnhnmland have been repeatedly cited as identical with Swift's. And this despite the fact that the incidents of the book show the author to be studiedly undercutting his hero-gull and to be using the metaphor of the rational *animal*, the Houyhnhnm, to make it plain that pure rationality is neither available nor appropriate to the human species—just as in the "Essay on Man" Pope's fully rational angels show "a Newton as we show an Ape.")

One aspect of the fictionality in Pope's case resides in the general plan of the formal satiric poem. This, as Miss Randolph has observed in the work of Horace, Persius, and Juvenal, contains always two layers. There is a thesis layer attacking vice and folly, elaborated with every kind of rhetorical device, and, much briefer, an antithesis layer illustrating or implying a philosophy of rational control, usually embodied in some more or less ideal norm like the Stoic *vir bonus*, the good plain man. The contours of formal verse satire, in other words, are not established entirely or even principally by a poet's rancorous sensibility; they are part of a fiction.

We encounter a further aspect of this fiction when we pause to consider that the bipartite structure just mentioned apparently exists to reflect a more general fictive situation. This situation is the warfare of good and evil—differentiated in satire from the forms it might take in, say, lyric, by being viewed from the angle of social solidarity rather than private introspection; and from the forms it might take in, say, tragedy, by being carried on in a context that asserts the primacy of moral decision, as tragedy asserts the primacy of moral understanding.

Tragedy and satire, I suspect, are two ends of a literary spectrum. Tragedy tends to exhibit the inadequacy of norms, to dissolve systematized values, to precipitate a meaning containing—but not necessarily contained by—recognizable ethical codes. Satire, on the contrary, asserts the validity and necessity of norms, systematic values, and meanings that *are* contained by recognizable codes. Where tragedy fortifies the sense of irrationality and complexity in experience because it presents us a world in which man is more victim than agent, in which our commodities prove to be our defects (and vice versa), and in which blindness and madness are likely to be symbols of insight, satire tends to fortify our feeling that life makes more immediate moral sense. In the world it offers us, madness and blindness are usually the emblems of vice and folly, evil and good are clearly distinguishable, criminals and fools are invariably responsible (therefore censurable), and standards of judgment are indubitable. All this, too, results from a slant of the glass, a fictional perspective on the real world—which, as we know, does not wholly correspond either with the tragic outlook or the satiric one.

Finally, we must note, among these general and pervasive aspects of fictionality in satire, the *ethos* of the satirist. Classical rhetoric, it is well to recall, divides the persuasive elements in any communication from one man to another into three sorts: the force of the arguments employed, the appeal to the interest and emotions of the hearer, and the weight of authority that comes from the hearer's estimate of the speaker's character, his *ethos*. For the satirist especially, the establishment of an au-

thoritative *ethos* is imperative. If he is to be effective in "that delightful teaching," he must be accepted by his audience as a fundamentally virtuous and tolerant man, who challenges the doings of other men not whenever he happens to feel vindictive, but whenever they deserve it. On this account, the satirist's *apologia* for his satire is one of the stock subjects of both the classical writers and Pope: the audience must be assured that its censor is a man of good will, who has been, as it were, *forced* into action. *Difficile est saturam non scribere:* "It is difficult *not* to write satire."

Moreover, the satirist's *ethos* is the *rhetorical* occasion (even though vanity may be among the *motives*) of his frequent citations of himself. As a candid fellow, for instance, and no pretender to be holier than thou:

> I love to pour out all myself, as plain
> As downright Shippen, or as old Montaigne. . . .
> In me what Spots, (for Spots I have) appear,
> Will prove at least the Medium must be clear.

A man, too, of simple tastes, persistent loyalties:

> Content with little, I can piddle here
> On Broccoli and mutton, round the Year;
> But ancient friends, (tho' poor, or out of play)
> That touch my Bell, I cannot turn away.

A man whose character was formed in the good old-fashioned way by home instruction and edifying books:

> Bred up at home, full early I begun
> To read in Greek, the Wrath of Peleus' Son.
> Besides, My Father taught me from a Lad,
> The better Art, to know the good from bad.

Consequently, a man who honors the natural pieties:

> Me, let the tender Office long engage
> To rock the Cradle of reposing Age:

who is sensible of life's true ends:

> Farewell then Verse, and Love, and ev'ry Toy,
> The rhymes and rattles of the Man or Boy,

What right, what true, what fit, we justly call,
Let this be all my Care—for this is All:

and who is valued by distinguished friends.
If the friends happen to be out of power,
or drawn in part from a vanished Golden
Age, so much the better for *ethos:* our satirist is guaranteed to be no time-server.

But does the Court a worthy Man remove?
That instant, I declare, he has my love.
I shun his Zenith, court his mild Decline;
Thus Sommers once, and Halifax were mine.
Oft in the clear, still Mirrour of Retreat
I study'd Shrewsbury, the wise and great. . . .
How pleasing Atterbury's softer hour!
How shin'd the Soul, unconquer'd in the Tow'r!
How can I Pult'ney, Chesterfield forget
While Roman Spirit charms, and Attic
Wit? . . .
Names which I long have lov'd, nor lov'd in
vain,
Rank'd with their Friends, not number'd with
their Train.

By passages of this kind in Pope's satires, the rhetorically innocent are habitually distressed. They remark with surprise
that Pope insists on portraying himself in
these poems as "lofty, good-humored,
calm, disinterested." Or they grow indignant that an epistle like "Arbuthnot" reveals "not what Pope really was, but what
he wished others to think him." They fail
to notice that he speaks this way only in a
certain kind of poem, and so enlarge irrelevantly—though to be sure with biographical truth enough—upon the subject
of his vanity. Meantime, on a rhetorical
view, the real point remains, which is simply that in passages of this sort, as also in
his notes to the "Dunciad," and probably,
to some extent, in the publication of his
letters (both these enterprises, signifi-
cantly, accompanied his turning satirist),
Pope felt the necessity of supporting the
ethos a satirical poet must have.

Obviously, the two agents to be considered in the fictive situation are the person
speaking and the person addressed. We
may, however, dismiss the second, for

though he is often a true *adversarius*—a
friend calculated like Job's friends to be
egregiously mistaken in his views and values—no one, I think, has ever seriously
misinterpreted a satire because he failed
to see that the *adversarius* was a fiction. It
is with the satiric speaker that the difficulty
has come. We may call this speaker Pope,
if we wish, but only if we remember that
he always reveals himself as a character in
a drama, not as a man confiding in us.
The distinction is apparent if we think of
Wordsworth's use of the word *young* in a
famous passage from "The Prelude" about
the early days of the French Revolution:
"Bliss was it in that dawn to be alive, And
to be young was very heaven"—and then
compare it with Pope's remark to the
friend with whom he professes to be con-
versing in the first dialogue of the "Epilogue to the Satires": "Dear Sir, forgive
the Prejudice of Youth." Wordsworth's
young is determined by something outside
the poem, something true (in the years to
which the poet refers) of himself in real
life. But in real life, when Pope wrote his
dialogue, he was already fifty; his *youth*
is true only of the satiric speaker of the
poem, who is an assumed identity, a
persona.

This *persona* or speaker has almost always in Pope's formal satires three distinguishable voices. One is the voice of the
man I have partly described in connection
with *ethos:* the man of plain living, high
thinking, lasting friendships; who hates
lies, slanders, lampoons; who laughs at
flatteries of himself; who is "soft by Nature, more a Dupe than Wit"; who loves
of all things best "the Language of the
Heart"; and who views his own poetry
with amused affection qualified with Vir-
gilian tenderness for the tears of things in
general:

Years foll'wing Years, steal something ev'ry
day,
At last they steal us from ourselves away;
In one our Frolicks, one Amusements end,

In one a Mistress drops, in one a Friend:
This subtle Thief of Life, this paltry Time,
What will it leave me, if it snatch my Rhime?

Then, secondly, there is the voice of the *naïf*, the *ingénu*, the simple heart: "the Prejudice of Youth." The owner of this voice is usually the vehicle of ironies about matters he professes not to understand, and is amazed by his own involvement in the literary arts. "I lisp'd in Numbers, for the Numbers came"—says this voice, speaking of one of the most carefully meditated poetries in literature. Or else: "Why did I write? What sin to me unknown Dipt me in Ink . . . ?" To the owner of this voice, his proficiency in satire is particularly puzzling. Should it be explained as the by-product of insomnia?

I nod in Company, I wake at Night,
Fools rush into my Head, and so I write;

a scheme of personal defense like jiujitsu?

Satire's my weapon . . .
Its proper pow'r to hurt each Creature feels,
Bulls aim their Horns, and Asses lift their
     Heels;

or is it a species of harmless madness, a kind of psychosomatic twitch that nothing short of death will stop?

Whether the darken'd Room to Muse invite,
Or whiten'd Wall provoke the Skew'r to write,
In Durance, Exile, Bedlam, or the Mint,
Like Lee and Budgell, I will Rhyme and Print.

Pope's third voice is that of the public defender. If the first voice gives us the satirist as *vir bonus,* the plain good private citizen, and the second, the satirist as *ingénu*, this one brings us the satirist as hero. A peculiar tightening in the verse takes place whenever this *persona* begins to speak, whether he speaks of the mysterious purposes of

That God of Nature, who, within us still.
Inclines our Action, not constrains our Will;

or of the time when

Inexorable Death shall level all,
And Trees, and Stones, and Farms, and Farmer
     fall;

or of his own calling:

Yes, I am proud; I must be proud to see
Men not afraid of God, afraid of me.

The satirist as *vir bonus* was content to laugh at flatteries, but the satirist as hero feels differently:

Fr. This filthy Simile, this beastly Line,
Quite turns my Stomach—P. So does Flatt'ry
     mine;
And all your Courtly Civet Cats can vent,
Perfume to you, to me is Excrement.

Similarly, the satirist as *ingénu* chose to find the motives of satire in a nervous reflex; the satirist as hero has other views:

O sacred Weapon! left for Truth's defence,
Sole dread of Folly, Vice, and Insolence!
To all but Heav'n-directed hands deny'd,
The Muse may give thee, but the Gods must
     guide.

Without pretending that these are the only voices Pope uses, or that they are always perfectly distinguishable, we may observe that the total dramatic development of any one of his formal satires is to a large extent determined by the way they succeed one another, modulate and qualify one another, and occasionally fuse with one another. In a poem like Pope's imitation of the first satire of Horace's second book, the structure is in a very real sense no more than a function of the modulations in tone that it takes to get from the opening verses, where the *naïf* shows up with his little slingshot and his five smooth pebbles from the brook:

Tim'rous by Nature, of the Rich in awe,
I come to Council learned in the Law;

through the point, about a hundred lines later, at which we realize that this fellow has somehow got Goliath's head in his hand (and also, the hero's accents in his voice):

Hear this, and tremble! you, who 'scape the Laws.
Yes, while I live, no rich or noble knave
Shall walk the World, in credit, to his grave;

then back down past a window opening on the unimpeachable integrity of the *vir bonus*, instanced in his ties with men whom it is no longer fashionable to know: "Chiefs, out of War, and Statesmen, out of Place"; and so, finally, to a reassumption of the voice of the *ingénu*, surprised and pained that he should be thought to have any but the noblest aims. "Libels and Satires!" he exclaims, on learning the category into which his poems are thrust— "lawless things indeed!"

But grave Epistles, bringing Vice to light,
Such as a King might read, a Bishop write,
Such as Sir Robert would approve ———?

Indeed? says the friend; well to be sure, *that's* different: "you may then proceed."

Though the construction in Pope's satires is by no means always so schematic as in this example, it seems almost invariably to invoke the three voices of the *naïf*, the *vir bonus*, and the hero. And their presence need not perhaps surprise us, if we pause to consider that they sum up, between them, most of what is essential in the satirist's position. As *naïf*, the satirist educates us. He makes us see the ulcer where we were accustomed to see the rouge. He is the child in the fairy story forever crying, "But mamma, the king *is* naked." As *vir bonus*, on the other hand, he wins our confidence in his personal moral insight. He shows us that he is stable, independent, urbane, wise—a man who knows there is a time to laugh, a time to weep: "Who would not weep, if Atticus were he?" And finally, as hero, he opens to us a world where the discernment of evil is always accompanied, as it is not always in the real world, by the courage to strike at it. He invites us, in an excellent phrase of Mr. Bredvold's,

to join "the invisible church of good men" everywhere, "few though they may be— for whom things matter." And he never lets us forget that we *are* at war; there *is* an enemy.

We should never have made, I think, so many mistakes about a portrait like "Sporus" if we had grasped the fact that it is primarily a portrait of the enemy (one of the finest Pope ever drew), evoked in a particular context at a particular point. We know, of course, that the lines were based on Pope's contemporary, Lord Hervey, whom he passionately disliked; and therefore we may justly infer that personal animus entered powerfully into their motivation.

But to read with this animus as our center of interest is to overlook the fact that, though the lines may be historically about Hervey, they are rhetorically about the enemy. It is to fail to see that they sum up in an *exemplum* (of which the implications become very pointed in the references to Satan) the fundamental attributes of the invader in every garden: his specious attractiveness—as a butterfly, a painted child, a dimpling stream; his nastiness—as a bug, a creature generated in dirt, a thing that stinks and stings, a toad spitting froth and venom; his essential impotence—as a mumbling spaniel, a shallow stream, a puppet, a hermaphrodite; and yet his perpetual menace as the tempter, powerless himself but always lurking "at the ear of Eve," as Pope puts it, to usurp the powers of good and pervert them. Because the lines associate Sporus with Evil in this larger sense, his portrait can be the ladder by which Pope mounts, in the evolution of the epistle as a whole, from the studiedly personal impatience of the pestered private citizen in the opening lines: " 'Shut, shut the door, good John!' fatigu'd I said," to the impersonal trumpet tones of the public defender on the walls of *Civitas Dei*— "Welcome for thee, fair Virtue, all the past." Without Sporus prostrate on the field behind him, the satiric speaker could never have supported this heroic tone. Something pretty close to the intensity exhibited by this portrait was called for, at just this point, not by the poet's actual feelings about a contemporary, but by the drama of feelings that has been building inside the poem—the fictive war—"the strong Antipathy of Good to Bad," here projected in its climactic symbol.

1810

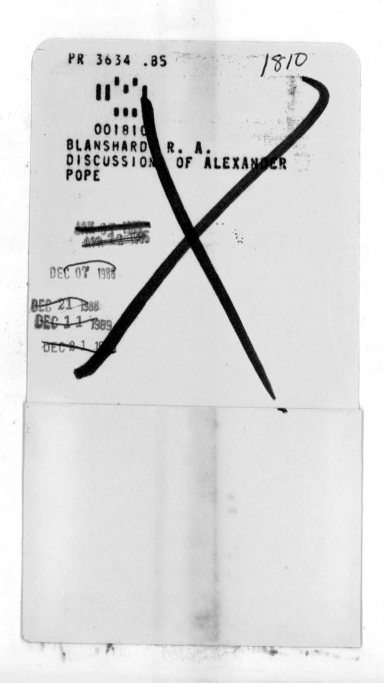